REMEMBER
and
RETURN

REMEMBER
and
RETURN

Rekindling Your Love
for the Savior—A Devotional

JOHN
MACARTHUR

BakerBooks
a division of Baker Publishing Group
Grand Rapids, Michigan

Published by Baker Books
a division of Baker Publishing Group
P.O. Box 6287, Grand Rapids, MI 49516-6287
www.bakerbooks.com

Printed in the United States of America

Adapted from *A Simple Christianity*, published by Regal Books, 2009.

Library of Congress Cataloging-in-Publication Data
Names: MacArthur, John, 1939– author.
Title: Remember and return : rekindling your love for the savior-a devotional / John MacArthur.
Description: Grand Rapids, MI : Baker Books, [2016] | Includes bibliographical references.
Identifiers: LCCN 2016005081 | ISBN 9780801019319 (cloth)
Subjects: LCSH: Jesus Christ—Person and offices—Meditations.
Classification: LCC BT203 .M265 2016 | DDC 232—dc23
LC record available at https://lccn.loc.gov/2016005081

16 17 18 19 20 21 22   7 6 5 4 3 2 1

In keeping with biblical principles of creation stewardship, Baker Publishing Group advocates the responsible use of our natural resources. As a member of the Green Press Initiative, our company uses recycled paper when possible. The text paper of this book is composed in part of post-consumer waste.

Contents

Preface

The Lord Jesus said, "If God were your Father, you would love Me" (John 8:42).

Thus did the divine Son of God identify the distinguishing mark of the children of God—love for the Lord Jesus. On the other hand, Scripture declares that souls doomed to judgment are cursed—because they do not love the Lord (see 1 Cor. 16:22).

The final benediction at the very end of Ephesians declares, "Grace be with all those who love our Lord Jesus Christ with incorruptible love" (Eph. 6:24), a love that is unfailing and immortal.

When Peter was caught and confronted in his disobedience by the Lord Jesus Himself, his gracious Savior asked him only one question—three times: "Do you love Me?" The dejected disciple answered that he did love the Lord, and the Lord knew his love was real because He knew Peter's heart (see John 21:15–17). This love for the risen Christ possesses the soul of every true Christian—as Peter said for all of us, "and though you have not seen Him, you love Him" (1 Pet. 1:8).

The believer's love for the Savior surpasses all loves on the human level, even the natural love of one's own life. This divine love, placed in the heart of every true believer by the Holy Spirit, is not merely a feeling. It is manifest in obedience.

> "He who has My commandments and keeps them is the one who loves Me; and he who loves Me will be loved by My Father, and I will love him and will disclose Myself to him." . . . Jesus answered and said to him, "If anyone loves Me, he will keep My word; and My Father will love him, and We will come to him and make Our abode with him." (John 14:21, 23)

Love for the Lord Jesus is the defining reality in the life of every true Christian. But the fire of the first love for the Lord can grow cold and diminish the believer's power and blessing. This thirty-one-day journey is designed to keep your love for Christ increasing for your joy and His glory.

Day 1
First Love

> I have this against you, that you have left your first love. There-
> fore remember from where you have fallen, and repent and do
> the deeds you did at first.
>
> Revelation 2:4–5

Loving the Lord Jesus Christ is what the Christian life is all about. If you are a Christian, you love Christ. Unfortunately your love is subject to fluctuation in its intensity. It takes a focused commitment on your part to love Him with all your heart, soul, mind, and strength.

There is perhaps no better illustration of this waning intensity than what happened to the church at Ephesus, to whom

Christ said, "I have this against you, that you have left your first love" (Rev. 2:4). The disease that plagued that congregation infects many contemporary churches. Instead of cultivating a deep and intimate relationship with Christ, many believers ignore Him, falling victim to the culture and turning to empty, worldly pursuits.

I am so concerned that love for Christ not grow cold in the lives of Christians that several times throughout my ministry at Grace Community Church I have preached a message of warning from Revelation 2:1–7. This passage crystallizes the danger of becoming so busy in activity for Christ that one forgets the necessity of maintaining a rich, loving relationship with Him. The church at Ephesus had a great beginning. The apostle Paul invested three years of his life teaching the Ephesian believers the whole counsel of God (see Acts 20:27, 31). Our Lord even commended the members for their service:

> I know your deeds and your toil and perseverance, and that you cannot tolerate evil men, and you put to the test those who call themselves apostles, and they are not, and you found them to be false; and you have perseverance and have endured for My name's sake, and have not grown weary. . . . You hate the deeds of the Nicolaitans, which I also hate. (Rev. 2:2–3, 6)

This was a noble group of people who worked hard and persevered through difficulty. They established holiness and righteousness as their standard. Because their doctrine was solid, they recognized false apostles and avoided their influence.

In spite of their success, they missed the most important thing—they left their first love. Their labor of passion and fervor became cold, orthodox, and mechanical. They left the heart out of their service—all their activity had become perfunctory. They believed and did all the right things but did so coldly.

Like Ephesus, the nation of Israel had been holy to the Lord at first. The Lord said to the people, "I remember concerning you the devotion of your youth, the love of your betrothals, your following after Me in the wilderness, through a land not sown" (Jer. 2:2). But then He said, "What injustice did your fathers find in Me, that they went far from Me?" (v. 5).

The honeymoon ended in Israel; it ended in Ephesus as well. Love turned cold is the forerunner of spiritual apathy, which then leads to a love for the world, compromise with evil, corruption, death, and finally judgment.

Can you imagine how you would feel if your husband or wife suddenly announced to you they didn't love you anymore yet they still planned to live with you and sleep with you, and nothing would change? Likewise you would never dream of telling the Lord you didn't love Him like you once did but you still planned to come to church to serve, sing, give, and worship Him. May I suggest, however, that you may be doing just that, only you don't realize it. That's the danger of spiritual apathy.

The apostle Paul never forgot the value of his relationship to Christ:

> Whatever things were gain to me, those things I have counted as loss for the sake of Christ. More than that, I count all things to be loss in view of the surpassing value of knowing Christ Jesus my Lord, for whom I have suffered the loss of all things, and count them but rubbish so that I may gain Christ. (Phil. 3:7–8)

Knowing Christ was his passion. For him nothing in life could capture his allegiance and devotion as much as Christ—not even his Hebrew heritage.

Ironically, Paul wanted to elicit the same love and devotion from the Ephesian believers. That's why he reminded them of their resources in Christ (see Eph. 1). We can't be sure how much they depended on Christ, but it must not have been enough, since our Lord had to command them, "Therefore remember from where you have fallen" (Rev. 2:5). A new generation had now risen in Ephesus that held to its strong tradition but not to an intense love for Christ. It's possible some were not even believers. Puritan Thomas Vincent recognized what a lack of love to Christ represents:

> The life of Christianity consists very much in our love to Christ. Without love to Christ, we are as much without spiritual life as a carcass when the soul is fled from it is without natural

life. Faith without love to Christ is a dead faith, and a Christian without love to Christ is a dead Christian, dead in sins and trespasses. Without love to Christ we may have the name of Christians, but we are wholly without the nature. We may have the form of godliness, but are wholly without the power.[1]

On the other hand, a true Christian is evident by his or her consuming love for Christ. Vincent continued:

If He has their love, their desires will be chiefly after Him. Their delights will be chiefly in Him; their hopes and expectations will be chiefly from Him. . . . Love will engage and employ for Him all the powers and faculties of their souls; their thoughts will be brought into captivity and obedience unto Him; their understandings will be employed in seeking and finding out His truths; their memories will be receptacles to retain them. . . .

All their senses and the members of their bodies will be His servants. Their eyes will see for Him, their ears will hear for Him, their tongues will speak for Him, their hands will work for Him, their feet will walk for Him. All their gifts and talents will be at His devotion and service. If He has their love, they will be ready to do for Him what He requires. They will suffer for Him whatever He calls them to. If they have much love to Him, they will not think much of denying themselves, taking up His cross, and following Him wherever He leads them.[2]

The Christian life is a continual pursuit of a deep, intimate relationship with Jesus Christ. Because we are committed to Christ, true Christians will do nothing to dishonor Him. Instead we will look to Him for mercy and grace when we sin. We will seek His strength during times of trial and temptation. And we will desire His wisdom and knowledge to lead us through the maze of life's confusing circumstances.

That's my goal for you in this devotional. Like our Lord's instruction for Ephesus, you need to remember what you have in Christ and what He has accomplished for you. In the following daily readings you will see Christ once again, as the God of the universe (days 2–7), as your loving Savior who willingly became a man to redeem you from God's wrath (days 8–17), and as the sovereign Lord who rules every part of your life (days 18–25). Hopefully this will rekindle your first love.

But our Lord's instruction for the church at Ephesus didn't stop with His command to remember. He also said, "Repent and do the deeds you did at first" (Rev. 2:5). Remembering who He is and how He has blessed you is not enough—you need to turn that knowledge into action (days 26–31).

Daily Challenge

Without making a concerted effort to change your direction, you'll never deepen your relationship with Christ.

Jettison the excess baggage you've picked up along the way and once again give Christ first place in your life. Don't "be led astray from the simplicity and purity of devotion to Christ" (2 Cor. 11:3), but exercise "love from a pure heart and a good conscience and a sincere faith" (1 Tim. 1:5).

Day 2
No Mere Man

> The Word became flesh, and dwelt among us, and we saw His glory, glory as of the only begotten from the Father, full of grace and truth.
>
> John 1:14

The One who is the object of our love was born contrary to the laws of nature, was reared in obscurity, lived in poverty, and only once crossed the boundary of the land in which He was born—and that was in His childhood. He had no wealth or influence and had neither training nor education in the world's schools. His relatives were inconspicuous and uninfluential.

In infancy He startled a king. In boyhood He puzzled learned doctors. In manhood He ruled the course of nature.

He walked upon the billows and hushed the sea to sleep. He healed the multitudes without medicine and made no charge for His services.

He never wrote a book, yet if everything He did were written in detail, the world itself couldn't contain the books that would be written. He never founded a college, yet all the schools together cannot boast of as many students as He has. He never practiced medicine, yet He has healed more broken hearts than doctors have healed broken bodies. Throughout history great men have come and gone, yet He lives on: Herod could not kill Him, Satan could not seduce Him, death could not destroy Him, and the grave could not hold Him.

But when the question is raised about who Jesus Christ really was, the debate continues to rage on as it has for nearly two thousand years. Cults and skeptics offer various explanations. Some say He was a religious fanatic, a fake, or a political revolutionary. Others say He was just a good teacher. Still others take an entirely different approach, saying He was the highest form of mankind, possessing a spark of divinity that He fanned into flame—a spark, they claim, we all have but seldom fan. Then there are those who believe Him to be one of many gods, a created being, a high angel, or a prophet.

The common thread of these countless human explanations is that they make Jesus less than God. Only God can tell us who He really was—and is. The biblical evidence contained in two passages—one written by the apostle Paul to a group of believers in Colossae (see Col. 1:15–19), the other written by an unknown author to Jewish believers and unbelievers (see Heb. 1:1–3)—offers us an overwhelming picture of the deity of Christ. Taken together, they leave no doubt that the man named Jesus, born of a virgin, was the incarnation of God and thus is worthy of our love and devotion.

Both the apostle Paul and the writer of Hebrews had specific goals in mind in declaring the deity of Christ. In the church at Colossae, Paul had to counteract the influence of what came to be known as *gnosticism*. Its adherents fancied themselves as having privileged access to some elevated mysteries they believed were truths so complex that common people couldn't understand them. They taught a form of philosophic dualism, postulating that spirit was good and matter was evil. They believed that because God is spirit, He is good, but that He could never touch matter, which is evil.

Therefore, they also concluded that God couldn't be the creator of the physical universe, because if God made matter, He would be responsible for evil. And they taught that God could never become a man, because as a man He would have to dwell in a body made of evil matter. So they explained away the incarnation by claiming that Jesus was a good angel whose body was only an illusion. But the apostle Paul said:

He is the image of the invisible God, the firstborn of all creation. For by Him all things were created, both in the heavens and on earth, visible and invisible, whether thrones or dominions or rulers or authorities—all things have been created through Him and for Him. He is before all things, and in Him all things hold together. He is also head of the body, the church; and He is the beginning, the firstborn from the dead, so that He Himself will come to have first place in everything. For it was the Father's good pleasure for all the fullness to dwell in Him. (Col. 1:15–19)

Paul specifically affirms Jesus as God in the flesh—the Creator of everything.

The writer of Hebrews, in contrast, was writing to Jews, some of whom did not believe Jesus to be the Messiah. In addition to affirming to Jewish believers the deity of Christ, he was trying to convince the unbelievers among them of Christ's superiority—His preeminence over any Old Testament person, institution, ritual, or sacrifice. The first three verses of chapter 1 are a summary of his entire epistle, weaving into a few brief words the superiority of Christ:

God, after He spoke long ago to the fathers in the prophets in many portions and in many ways, in these last days has spoken to us in His Son, whom He appointed heir of all things, through whom also He made the world. And He is the radiance of His glory and the exact representation of His nature, and upholds all things by the word of His power. (Heb. 1:1–3)

Jesus was no mere man. Those two passages declare that He was and is the preeminent One—the climax of God's revelation. Jesus Christ is the full representation of and the human expression of God—superior to and exalted above anyone or anything. If we are ever to return to our first love, we must base our relationship with Him on that irrefutable fact.

What should our response be to these glorious truths? Puritan John Owen astutely observed:

The revelation made of Christ in the blessed gospel is far more excellent, more glorious, more filled with rays of divine wisdom and goodness than the whole creation, and the just comprehension of it, if attainable, can contain or afford. Without this knowledge, the mind of man, however priding itself in other inventions and discoveries, is wrapped up in darkness and confusion.

This therefore deserves the severest of our thoughts, the best of our meditations, and our utmost diligence in them. For if our future blessedness shall consist in living where He is, and beholding of His glory, what better preparation can there be for it than a constant previous contemplation of that glory as revealed in the gospel, that by a view of it we may be gradually transformed into the same glory?[1]

Daily Challenge

Over the next two days we will continue, with the help of the apostle Paul and the author of Hebrews, to delve into the absolute supremacy of Jesus. Open yourself willingly to absorb His glory as God's Word reveals our beloved and exalted Christ. And may you be transformed by the encounter.

Day 3
Christ
and the Father

He is the image of the invisible God, the firstborn of all creation. For by Him all things were created, both in the heavens and on earth, visible and invisible, whether thrones or dominions or rulers or authorities—all things have been created through Him and for Him. He is before all things, and in Him all things hold together. He is also head of the body, the church; and He is the beginning, the firstborn from the dead, so that He Himself will come to have first place in everything. For it was the Father's good pleasure for all the fullness to dwell in Him.

Colossians 1:15–19

Those who dispute the deity of Christ sometimes attempt to use Colossians 1:15–19 to support their view. They suggest, for example, that the phrase "the image of the invisible God" (v. 15) indicates that Jesus was merely a created being who bore the image of God in the same sense as all humanity. But the Greek word translated "image" here is *eikon*, which refers to a perfect replica, a precise copy, or an exact reproduction, as in a fine sculpture or portrait. Paul was saying that God Himself is fully manifest in the Person of His Son, who is none other than Jesus Christ. He is the *exact* image of God.

Hebrews 1:3 makes an identical affirmation: "He is the radiance of His glory and the exact representation of His nature." Christ is to God as the warm brilliance of light is to the sun. Just as the sun is never without its brightness, so it is with Christ and God. They cannot be divided, and neither has ever existed without the other. They are one (see John 10:30).

The Greek word translated "radiance" (*apaugasma*, "to send forth light") represents Jesus as the manifestation of God. Since no one can see God at any time (see John 1:18), and none of us on earth ever will, the only radiance that reaches us from God is mediated to us from Jesus Christ.

We live in a world full of injustice, failure, privation, separation, disease, and death. A moral darkness covers men and women, who are blinded by their godless appetites and passions. The apostle Paul confirmed this fact: "Even if our gospel is veiled, it is veiled to those who are perishing, in whose case the god of this world has blinded the minds of the unbelieving so that they might not see the light of the gospel of the glory of Christ, who is the image of God" (2 Cor. 4:3–4).

But if you are Christian, God has opened your eyes to the light: "For God, who said, 'Light shall shine out of darkness,' is the One who has shone in our hearts to give the Light of the knowledge of the glory of God in the face of Christ" (v. 6). Jesus Himself said, "I am the Light of the world; he who follows Me will not walk in the darkness, but will have the Light of life" (John 8:12). We would never be able to see or enjoy God's light if we couldn't see Jesus. His light is life itself—true spiritual life, which gives us purpose, meaning, peace, joy, and fellowship for all eternity.

Hebrews 1:3 also says that Christ is "the exact representation of [God's] nature." Jesus is the express image of God not only in His manifestation but also in His very essence or substance. Even in His incarnation He set aside the use of His attributes, not the attributes themselves, so He was always fully God. "He who has seen Me," He told the disciples, "has seen the Father" (John 14:9). Paul confirmed that the glory of God shines in Jesus Christ (see 2 Cor. 4:4, 6).

"Exact representation" translates the Greek word *charakter*, from which we derive the English words *character* and *characteristic*. The Greeks typically used this term for an impression made by a die or stamp on a seal, in which the design on the die is reproduced on the wax. By using such terminology, the writer of Hebrews was claiming that Jesus Christ is the reproduction of God—the perfect, personal imprint of God in time and space.

Through Christ the invisible God has been made visible. God's full likeness is revealed in Him. Colossians 1:19 takes the truth a step further: "It was the Father's good pleasure for all the fullness to dwell in Him." He is not just an outline of God; He is fully God. Colossians 2:9 is even more explicit: "In Him all the fullness of Deity dwells in bodily form." Nothing is lacking. No attribute is absent. He is God in the fullest possible sense.

In Colossians 1:15 Paul said Jesus is "the firstborn of all creation." Those who reject the deity of Christ have made much of that phrase, assuming it means Jesus was a created being and thus He could not be the eternal God. But the word translated "firstborn" (*prototokos*) describes Jesus's rank, not His origin. Although *prototokos* can mean firstborn chronologically (see Luke 2:7), it refers primarily to position. In both Greek and Jewish culture, the firstborn was the son who ranked first and thus had the right of inheritance. As a result, the firstborn son in a royal family had the right to rule. Christ is the One who inherits all creation and the right to rule over it.

In Psalm 89:27 God said of David, "I also shall make [you] My firstborn, the highest of the kings of the earth." There the meaning of "firstborn" is given in plain language: "the highest of the kings of the earth." That's what *prototokos* means with regard to Christ—He is "Lord of lords and King of kings" (Rev. 17:14).

Hebrews 1 again offers a parallel statement; verse 2 says God has appointed His Son "heir of all things." As the Son of God, Jesus is the heir of all that God possesses. Everything that exists in the universe will find its true meaning only when it comes under His control. We see that theme in Psalms, where the Father says to the Son, "Ask of Me, and I will surely give the nations as Your inheritance, and the very ends of the earth as Your possession" (2:8).

In the last days, God's kingdom will be given finally and eternally to Jesus Christ (see Rev. 11:15). Revelation 5 pictures God in heaven sitting on a throne, holding a sealed scroll in His hand. That scroll is the title deed to the earth and all that's in it. And He is holding it for the Heir—the One who has the right to possess the earth.

Roman law required that a will be sealed seven times to protect it from being tampered with, and that is true of this title deed. At first no one is found worthy to break its seals. But Jesus Christ, the worthy Lamb, comes and takes the scroll from the right hand of God because He—and He alone—has the right to do so.

Revelation 6 records the first step in Christ's taking back the earth that is rightfully His. As He breaks each seal, one by one,

He takes further possession and control of His inheritance. Finally, when He breaks the seventh seal, the seventh trumpet blows, and the seventh bowl is poured out, the earth is His.

When Christ first came to earth, He became poor so that we through His poverty might be made rich (see 2 Cor. 8:9). He had nothing for Himself, "nowhere to lay His head" (Luke 9:58). Even His clothes were taken from Him when He died, and He was buried in a borrowed grave. But when Christ comes again, things will be different. He will completely and eternally inherit all things.

Those who trust their lives to Him will be fellow heirs with Him (see Rom. 8:16–17). When we enter His eternal kingdom, we will jointly possess all that He possesses. We will not be joint Christs or Lords, but we will be joint heirs of His marvelous inheritance.

Daily Challenge

Since Jesus Christ is the image of God, has the right to rule the earth, and one day will make us joint heirs of His inheritance, we owe Him our undying love and devotion. Those truths alone ought to make us return to our first love.

Day 4
The Preeminent One

God, after He spoke long ago to the fathers in the prophets in many portions and in many ways, in these last days has spoken to us in His Son, whom He appointed heir of all things, through whom also He made the world. And He is the radiance of His glory and the exact representation of His nature, and upholds all things by the word of His power.

Hebrews 1:1–3

We've seen that Jesus Christ is fully divine and therefore God the Father's rightful heir to the universe. Paul and the author of Hebrews continue to unveil several more implications of these realities. Colossians 1:16–17 explicitly names Christ as Creator of everything: "For by Him all things were created, both in the heavens and on earth, visible and invisible, whether thrones or dominions or rulers or authorities—all things have been created through Him and for Him. He is before all things." He is not part of creation; He is the Creator, the very arm of God, active from the beginning in calling the universe and all creatures into existence. John 1:3 says, "All things came into being through Him, and apart from Him nothing came into being that has come into being." That could not be true if He were Himself a created being.

Hebrews 1:2 also identifies Christ as the Creator. He is the Person of the Trinity "through whom also [God] made the world," and for whom it was fashioned. One of the greatest proofs of Jesus's divinity is His power to create everything material and everything spiritual.

Think of what that means. The expanse of creation is staggering. Have you ever reflected on the size of the universe? If it doesn't impress on you the majesty of God, you haven't really considered it.

A ray of light travels 186,000 miles per second, so a beam of light from here will reach the moon in a second and a half. Imagine traveling that fast. It would take four years and four months to make it to the nearest star. Traveling across our galaxy, the Milky Way, would take you about one hundred thousand years. If you could count the stars as you travel, they would number about one hundred billion in the Milky Way alone. If you wanted to explore other galaxies, you would have billions to choose from.

Where did it all come from? Who conceived it? Who made it? It can't be an accident, and the Bible tells us its maker is Jesus Christ. Jesus holds primacy over creation because "He is before all things" (Col. 1:17). When the universe began, He already existed (see John 1:1–2; 1 John 1:1). He told the Jews in John 8:58, "Before Abraham was born, I am." He identified Himself as Yahweh, the eternally existing God. The prophet Micah said of Him, "His goings forth are from long ago, from the days of eternity" (Mic. 5:2).

Furthermore, Paul added that "in Him all things hold together" (Col. 1:17). The author of Hebrews confirmed Paul's declaration: Christ "upholds all things by the word of His power" (1:3). The Greek word translated "upholds" means "to support or maintain." It's used here in the present tense, implying continuous action. Everything in the universe is being sustained right now by Jesus Christ. He maintains the delicate balance necessary to life's existence by quite literally holding all things together. He keeps all the entities in space in motion. He is the power behind every consistency in the universe.

Can you imagine what would happen if Christ relinquished His sustaining power over the laws of the universe? If just one of the physical laws varied, we could not exist. Consider the resulting destruction if the earth's rotation slowed just a little, or if it moved any closer to or farther from the sun. How does our world maintain such a fantastically delicate balance? Through Jesus Christ, who sustains and monitors all its movements. The universe is a cosmos, not a chaos—an ordered, reliable system instead of an erratic, unpredictable muddle—only because Jesus Christ upholds it all. Knowing that, how could any Christian not bow before Him to love and adore Him?

Christ also is the creator of "thrones," "dominions," "rulers," and "authorities" (Col. 1:16). Those terms refer to the various ranks of angels Christ created. The writer of Hebrews also made a clear distinction between Christ and the angels: "Of the angels He says, 'Who makes His angels winds, and His ministers a flame of fire.' But of the Son He says, 'Your throne, O God, is forever and ever, and the righteous scepter is the scepter of His kingdom'" (Heb. 1:7–8).

Scripture is clear that Jesus is not an angel but the Creator and Master of the angels. Jesus's relation to the unseen spiritual world, like His relation to the visible universe, proves He is God.

Paul continued his treatise on the preeminence of Christ with four great realities about His relationship to the church: "He is also head of the body, the church; and He is the beginning, the firstborn from the dead; so that He Himself will come to have first place in everything" (Col. 1:18).

First, He is the head. Scripture uses the metaphor of the human body to describe the church, and that means Christ is the head of the body. The church is not merely an organization; it is a living organism, controlled by the living Christ. He rules every part of it and gives it life and direction. Because He lives His life through all the members, He produces unity in the body (see 1 Cor. 12:12–20). He energizes and coordinates diversity within the body, a diversity manifested in spiritual gifts and ministries (see vv. 4–13). He also directs the body's mutuality, as the individual members serve and support each other (see vv. 15–27).

Second, He is the beginning. *Arche* ("beginning") refers to source, rank, or primacy. It can also be translated "chief" or "pioneer." Since Christ is both the source of the church and its chief, the church has its origins in Him. God "chose us in Him before the foundation of the world" (Eph. 1:4). As Head of the body, Jesus holds the highest rank in the church. As the beginning of it, He is its originator.

Third, He is the firstborn from the dead. Earlier we discussed the meaning of "firstborn." Of all those who have been raised from the dead, or ever will be, Christ is the greatest.

Fourth, He is the preeminent One. Much is made of acquiring first place in our day. From sports to business, the goal of teams and corporations is to be number one. But there is only One who truly holds first place. As a result of His death and resurrection, Jesus has first place in everything.

As we conclude three days of examining the absolute supremacy of Jesus Christ, we consider Paul's summation of his argument in Colossians 1:15–19: "For it was the Father's good pleasure for all the fullness to dwell in Him" (v. 19). *Pleroma* ("fullness") was a term used by the later gnostics to refer to the divine powers and attributes, which they believed were divided among various emanations. Paul's point was that all the fullness of deity is not spread out in small doses to a group of spirits but fully dwells in Christ alone (see 2:9). In Christ, and in Him alone, we are complete (see v. 10). Christians share in His fullness: "For of His fullness we have all received, and grace upon grace" (John 1:16). All the fullness of Christ becomes available to those who place their trust in Him.

God says His Son has first place in all things. What does that mean to you? It ought to mean everything. To reject Him is to be shut out of His presence into an eternal hell. But to receive Him is to enter into all that He is and has—there are no other choices.

Daily Challenge

If you are to ever regain your first love, it is absolutely necessary for you to acknowledge that Jesus does in fact have first place in everything, including your life. You do not occupy a position of prominence; only He does. The sooner you recognize that, the quicker you will begin to reestablish your love for Him.

Day 5
Chosen in Christ

Those whom He foreknew, He also predestined to become conformed to the image of His Son, so that He would be the firstborn among many brethren.

Romans 8:29

Man is morally and spiritually bankrupt. Nothing he can do will ever produce righteousness or give him value. Romans 3:10–12 gives us the reason: "There is none righteous, not even one; there is none who understands, there is none who seeks for God; all have turned aside, together they have become useless; there is none who does good, there is not even one." All efforts at establishing self-righteousness are doomed to fail because man on his own is incapable of doing good.

Genuine meaning and purpose can only come out of a right relationship to the Creator. The apostle John wrote of Jesus, "But as many as received Him, to them He gave the right to become children of God, even to those who believe in His name, who were born, not of blood nor of the will of the flesh nor of the will of man, but of God" (John 1:12–13). There is no greater value than realizing that you were specially chosen by God to be a part of His family. Nothing can compare to that.

Ephesians 1:3–6, which we will take three days to explore, is a record of God's role in our salvation and what He has made available to us through His Son. These verses take us back to eternity past, letting us eavesdrop on God's plan to save us—not only long before we were born but also before the earth was born. Paul wrote:

> Blessed be the God and Father of our Lord Jesus Christ, who has blessed us with every spiritual blessing in the heavenly places in Christ, just as He chose us in Him before the foundation of the world, that we would be holy and blameless before Him. In love He predestined us to adoption as sons through Jesus Christ to Himself, according to the kind intention of His will, to the praise of the glory of His grace. (Eph. 1:3–6)

While God is the focus of those verses, you need to understand the role Christ has in carrying out God's salvation plan.

It is through our union with Him that we receive salvation and the blessings of God.

The dictionary defines an agent as "one empowered to act for or represent another." Some of the most powerful people in the entertainment and sports industries are the high-priced agents who represent famous celebrities or athletes. You're probably more familiar with lower-profile agents, such as an insurance agent who represents the insured and the insurance company, or a real estate agent who represents a buyer and seller.

In a similar fashion, Christ is God's agent when it comes to salvation. Notice these phrases from Ephesians 1: we have been blessed "with every spiritual blessing in the heavenly places *in* Christ," "He chose us *in* Him," and "He predestined us to adoption as sons *through* Jesus Christ to Himself" (vv. 3–5, emphases added).

When we trust in Christ as our Lord and Savior, we are placed into a marvelous union with Him. First Corinthians 6:17 says, "The one who joins himself to the Lord is one spirit with Him." Our unity with Christ is more than simply common agreement—it is the deep, internal commonness of sharing eternal life with God.

Romans 8:16–17 says, "We are children of God, and if children, heirs also, heirs of God and fellow heirs with Christ." Because we are one in Jesus Christ, His righteousness is imputed to us and His inheritance—all of God's riches—is ours.

His position is now our position, His privilege is now our privilege, His possessions are now our possessions, and His practice is now our practice. We are significant not because of who we are but because of what we become in Christ.

Our relationship to Christ takes on added significance when we realize that we are a gift from God to His Son. Christ understood that when He said to the Father, "I have manifested Your name to the men whom You gave Me out of the world; they were Yours and You gave them to Me, and they have kept Your word" (John 17:6). Regarding this topic, D. Martyn Lloyd-Jones wrote:

> These people . . . belonged to God before they became the Son's people. Our position does not depend upon anything we do, primarily; nor primarily even upon the action of the Son. The primary action is that of God the Father who chose unto Himself a people out of the whole of mankind before the foundation of the world, and then presented, gave these people whom He had chosen to the Son, in order that the Son might redeem them and do everything that was necessary for their reconciliation with Himself. That is the teaching of the Lord Jesus Christ Himself. He came into the world, and accomplished His work, for these people who have been given to Him by the Father. . . . But it is of vital importance that we should remember that it is all done "in Him." The apostle continually repeats the truth that there is nothing whatsoever given to the Christian apart

from the Lord Jesus Christ; there is no relationship to God which is true and saving except that which is in and through the Son of God. "There is one God, and one mediator [only] between God and men, the man Christ Jesus" (1 Tim. 2:5).[1]

The gift God promised (see 2 Tim. 1:9; Titus 1:2) to give the Son was a redeemed humanity that would ultimately glorify Him for what He had done. Romans 8:29 reveals how that works out in God's ultimate purpose for our salvation: "Whom He foreknew, He also predestined to become conformed to the image of His Son, so that He would be the firstborn among many brethren."

From before time began, God chose to save believers from their sins that they might "become conformed to the image of His Son," Jesus Christ. Consequently, every true believer moves inexorably toward perfection in righteousness, as God makes for Himself a people re-created in the likeness of His own divine Son (see Gal. 4:19; Col. 1:28; 1 John 3:2), who will dwell and reign with Him in heaven throughout all eternity. God is redeeming for Himself an eternally holy and Christlike race, to be citizens in His divine kingdom and children in His divine family.

Ultimately, though, God's supreme purpose for bringing sinners to salvation is to glorify His Son by making Him pre-eminent in the divine plan of redemption. It is God's intent for Christ to "be the firstborn among many brethren" (Rom.

8:29). As we noted earlier, "firstborn" was often used in Jewish culture figuratively to represent preeminence. That is its meaning in the present context.

As it is in almost every instance in the New Testament, the term *brethren* is synonymous with "believers." God's primary purpose in His plan of redemption was to make His beloved Son "the firstborn among many brethren" in the sense of Christ's being uniquely preeminent among the children of God. Those who trust in Him become God's adopted children, and Jesus, the Son of God, graciously calls them His brothers and sisters in God's divine family (see Matt. 12:50).

Daily Challenge

God's purpose is to make us like Christ to create a great redeemed and glorified humanity over which He will reign and be forever preeminent. Thus our ultimate purpose as the redeemed children of God will be to spend eternity worshiping and giving praise to God's beloved "firstborn," our preeminent Lord and Savior, Jesus Christ. Paul referred to that purpose as "the prize of the upward call of God" (Phil. 3:14), meaning the reward of heaven. That was "the goal" Paul strived for in this life, and it certainly ought to be the focus of those who would return to their first love.

Day 6
The Blessings of Our Salvation

Blessed be the God and Father of our Lord Jesus Christ, who has blessed us with every spiritual blessing in the heavenly places in Christ.

Ephesians 1:3

A Christian is a child of God and a joint heir with Christ, having been chosen in Christ before the foundation of the world (see Eph. 1:4). The record of God's redemptive history is that of His reaching down and drawing to Himself those whom He has chosen to save. As Christians we have significance to fulfill the divine purpose only by knowing God and His Son, realizing that apart from any inherent value in us, and out of grace and in divine sovereignty, He chose each one of us to belong to Him.

Along with this privilege, God made provision for everything we need in order to live according to His design. Let's turn to Paul's discussion of what God the Father planned for His children. It begins in Ephesians 1, where we learn of the tremendous blessings available to those who are saved. Paul started by praising the One who has provided the blessing: "Blessed be the God and Father of our Lord Jesus Christ" (v. 3). The Greek word translated "blessed" is *eulogetos*, from which we derive the English word *eulogy*. It is a declaration of an individual's goodness.

The Bible records the goodness of God from beginning to end. Melchizedek declared, "Blessed be God Most High" (Gen. 14:20). In the last days "every created thing which is in heaven and on the earth and under the earth and on the sea, and all things in them [will be] heard saying, 'To Him who sits on the throne, and to the Lamb, be blessing and honor and glory and dominion forever and ever'" (Rev. 5:13).

Consistent with His perfection and praiseworthiness, the One who is to be supremely blessed for His goodness is Himself the One "who has blessed us." James said that, "every good thing given and every perfect gift is from above, coming down from the Father of lights, with whom there is no variation or shifting shadow" (James 1:17). Romans 8:28 says, "God causes all things to work together for good to those who love God, to those who are called according to His purpose." God is good and blesses because He is the source of every good thing.

The recipients of God's blessing are believers. In His marvelous providence, wonderful grace, and sovereign plan, God has chosen to be eternally good to us. When we praise His goodness, we bless Him. When He blesses us, He communicates good to us. We bless Him with words; He blesses us with deeds. Our heavenly Father lavishes us with every good gift. That is His nature, and that is our need.

Paul next told us that we have been blessed "with all spiritual blessings." Unfortunately, most believers are unaware of the extent of those blessings and are constantly asking God for things He has already provided. They pray for such things as love, peace, joy, and strength, when all the while those very blessings are theirs for the taking (e.g., John 14:27; 15:11; Rom. 5:5; Phil. 4:13). God has given us all spiritual blessings, yet we need to ask for wisdom in understanding how to use those resources (see James 1:5).

There are no missing ingredients in God's blessing. It is not that God *will* give but that He has *already* given us "everything pertaining to life and godliness" (2 Pet. 1:3). He has blessed us already with every spiritual blessing. Our resources in Christ are not simply promised to us; they are actually in our possession. Every believer has what Paul called "the provision of the Spirit of Jesus Christ" (Phil. 1:19). God cannot give us more than He has already given us in Christ—we are complete in Him (see Col. 2:10). The believer's need, therefore, is not to receive something more but to do something more with what he or she has.

Our abundant, unlimited resources and realities reside "in the heavenly places," an area that encompasses the entire supernatural realm of God. While it includes heaven, it's not limited to that. It refers to all things that are transcendent, eternal, and spiritual—love, forgiveness, peace—all those elements that reside only in the kingdom of God. This is no promise of health, wealth, and success in this world. Just the opposite; it is the promise of things not of this world.

Christians are not so much citizens of the earth as they are citizens of heaven. Philippians 3:20 says plainly, "Our citizenship is in heaven, from which also we eagerly wait for a Savior, the Lord Jesus Christ." Because we are citizens of heaven, we are able to understand the supernatural things of God, things that the "natural man does not accept" and "cannot understand . . . because they are spiritually appraised" (1 Cor. 2:14).

When an American citizen travels abroad, he remains as much an American citizen as when he is in the United States. Whether he is in Africa, the Near East, Europe, or anywhere outside his homeland, he is still an American citizen and possesses all the rights and privileges that accompany his citizenship.

As citizens of God's heavenly kingdom, Christians possess all the rights and privileges that citizenship grants (some present, some future), even while they are living in the "foreign" and hostile environment of earth. Our true life is in heaven—our Father, Savior, family, loved ones, and home are there. While there is much we long for in heaven, we must continue our sojourn on earth for as long as the Lord wills.

The key to living as heavenly citizens while living in this world is to walk by the Spirit, and in so doing, Paul said, we "will not carry out the desire of the flesh" (Gal. 5:16). Instead, we will be the beneficiaries of the fruit of the Spirit (see vv. 22–23). We receive our blessings by living in the power of the Spirit.

If you are ever tempted to let earthly pursuits become the priority in your life, remember the abundance of blessings God has for you. Then you'll be sure to hang on to your first love.

Daily Challenge

As you can see, our purpose comes from knowing that we are the object of God's love and that He chose us to be members of His divine family. Since you are a child of the King, you have become precious to Him. And because God has given us all spiritual blessings in the heavenlies, we have an unlimited supply of divine resources. Be sure to use them to make your life fulfilling, to minister with the greatest amount of power, and to fulfill the purpose of the church that Jesus purchased with His precious blood.

Day 7
God's Plan
from Eternity Past

He chose us in Him before the foundation of the world, that we would be holy and blameless before Him. In love He predestined us to adoption as sons through Jesus Christ to Himself, according to the kind intention of His will, to the praise of the glory of His grace.

Ephesians 1:4–6

We now travel back in time, long before any of us were born, even before Adam was raised from the dust. In fact, we are privileged, through the inspired words of the apostle Paul, to glimpse the deliberations and preparations of the Trinity prior to creation, as God established the eternal plan of salvation.

The Bible teaches three kinds of election. One is God's theocratic election of Israel (see Deut. 7:6). But that had no bearing on personal salvation. Racial descent from Abraham as father of the Hebrew people did not mean spiritual descent from him as father of the faithful (see Rom. 4:11).

The second kind of election is vocational. The Lord called out the tribe of Levi to be His priests, but they were not guaranteed salvation. Jesus chose twelve men as apostles, yet Judas Iscariot was not a believer.

The third kind of election is salvational, the type Paul was referring to in Ephesians 1:4. Jesus explained, "No one can come to Me unless the Father who sent Me draws him" (John 6:44). No one is saved unless he is drawn (*helkuo*). That term is used in nonbiblical writings to speak of an irresistible force. This drawing force of God can be likened to an electromagnet that draws iron while leaving nonferrous metal unmoved. God's election is irresistible to those upon whom He has set His love. The elect will respond in faith to the divine magnet.

Completely apart from any merit of any individual, by God's sovereign election, those who are saved were placed in eternal union with Christ Jesus before creation even took place.

Although man's will is not free in the sense that many people suppose, it is still part of his being. Apart from God, that will is captive to sin. But he still has the capacity and responsibility to choose God because God makes that choice possible. And only God can do it, because if left to our own abilities, we could never choose Him (see Rom. 3:11).

Jesus said that whoever believes in Him will not perish but have eternal life (see John 3:16) and that "everyone who lives and believes in Me will never die" (11:26). The frequent commands to the unsaved to respond to the Lord (i.e., Matt. 3:1–2; 4:17; Mark 1:14–15) clearly indicate the responsibility of man to exercise his own will. Yet the Bible is just as clear that no person receives Jesus Christ as Savior and Lord who has not been chosen by God (see Rom. 8:29; 1 Pet. 1:2).

God's sovereign election and man's exercise of responsibility in choosing Jesus Christ seem opposite and irreconcilable truths. In his book *Evangelism and the Sovereignty of God*, J. I. Packer warned of the dangers of attempting to reconcile them:

> People see the Bible teaches man's responsibility for his actions; they do not see . . . how this is consistent with the sovereign Lordship of God over those actions. They are not content to let the two truths live side by side, as they do in the Scriptures, but jump to the conclusion that, in order to uphold the biblical truth of human responsibility, they are bound to reject the equally biblical and equally true doctrine of divine sovereignty, and to explain away the great number of texts that teach it. The

desire to oversimplify the Bible by cutting out the mysteries
is natural. . . . Hence this persistent and troublesome dispute.
The irony of the situation, however, is that when we ask how
the two sides pray, it becomes apparent that those who profess
to deny God's sovereignty really believe in it just as strongly
as those who affirm it.[1]

Divine sovereignty and human responsibility are integral
and inseparable realities of salvation—though exactly how
they operate together only the infinite mind of God knows.

God elected us "before the foundation of the world." Before
the creation of the universe we were sovereignly predestined
by God to be His. The apostle Peter declared that we were
redeemed "with precious blood, as of a lamb unblemished and
spotless, the blood of Christ. For He was foreknown before
the foundation of the world" (1 Pet. 1:19–20). Just as Christ's
crucifixion was planned out before the world began, so we
were designated for salvation by that same plan at that same
time. It was then that our inheritance in God's kingdom was
determined (see Matt. 25:34). Our names were "written from
the foundation of the world in the book of life of the Lamb
who has been slain" (Rev. 13:8).

Paul said that God's purpose was so that we might be "holy
and blameless" (Eph. 1:4). Paul also said we were "predestined
to become conformed to the image of His Son" (Rom. 8:29).
Because Christ gave Himself for us as "a lamb unblemished

and spotless" (1 Pet. 1:19), God has given us His own unblemished and spotless nature. The unworthy have been declared
worthy, the unrighteous declared holy.

Our practice is far from Christlike and far from blameless. Yet in Colossians 2:10 Paul said, "In Him [we] have been
made complete." That's why our salvation is secure—we have
Christ's perfect righteousness. Our practice can and does fall
short, but our position can never fall short because it is the
same holy and blameless position Christ has before God. And
because God has declared us to be holy and blameless, we
should strive to reflect that in our lives by pursuing the very
image of Christ (see Phil. 3:9–14) as we live in this world.

God chose us to be His children because of His love (see
John 3:16). Biblical *agape* love is not an emotion; it is an act
of self-sacrifice on behalf of others. The preeminent expression of God's love is the death of His Son: "Greater love has
no one than this, that one lay down his life for his friends"
(John 15:13). In the ultimate divine act of love, God determined before the foundation of the earth that He would give
His only Son to save us. Paul said, "God, being rich in mercy,
because of His great love with which He loved us, even when
we were dead in our transgressions, made us alive together
with Christ" (Eph. 2:4–5).

The result of God's election is that "He predestined us to
adoption as sons through Jesus Christ to Himself" (1:5). In

His great love He makes us more than citizens and servants, and even more than friends—He makes us children, lovingly drawing us into the intimacy of His own family.

We became His children the instant we were saved (see John 1:12). In fact, as His children, we can now address God in an intimate way—"Abba," the Aramaic equivalent of "Daddy" (Gal. 4:6). Our adoption means that the life of God dwells in us. We actually are "partakers of the divine nature" (2 Pet. 1:4) in that the Spirit of God dwells in us (see Gal. 4:6). Why did God do all this for us? Paul said it was "according to the kind intention of His will, to the praise of the glory of His grace" (Eph. 1:5–6). Above all else, He elects and saves us for His own glory.

Daily Challenge

God chose and preordained who would be conformed to the image of Christ before the foundation of the world so that no human beings could boast or take glory for themselves but that all the credit might be His. Salvation is all from God, and therefore all the glory belongs to Him. The ultimate reason for everything that exists is the honor of the Almighty. That is why, as God's children, Christians should do everything they do "to the glory of God" (1 Cor. 10:31).

Day 8
The God-Man

Have this attitude in yourselves which was also in Christ Jesus,
who, although He existed in the form of God, did not regard
equality with God a thing to be grasped.

Philippians 2:5–6

British author C. S. Lewis, in the chapter "The Grand Miracle"
from his book *Miracles*, described the incarnation of Christ
in this manner:

In the Christian story God descends to re-ascend. He comes
down; down from the heights of absolute being into time and
space, down into humanity . . . down to the very roots and
sea-bed of the Nature He has created.

But He goes down to come up again and bring the ruined world up with Him. One has the picture of a strong man stooping lower and lower to get himself underneath some great complicated burden. He must stoop in order to lift, he must almost disappear under the load before he incredibly straightens his back and marches off with the whole mass swaying on his shoulders. . . .

In this descent and re-ascent everyone will recognise a familiar pattern: a thing written all over the world. It is the pattern of all vegetable life. It must belittle itself into something hard, small and deathlike, it must fall into the ground: thence the new life re-ascends. . . .

So it is also in our moral and emotional life. The first innocent and spontaneous desires have to submit to the deathlike process of control or total denial: but from that there is a re-ascent to fully formed character in which the strength of the original material all operates but in a new way. Death and Rebirth—go down to go up—it is a key principle. Through this bottleneck, this belittlement, the highroad nearly always lies.[1]

What Lewis described so eloquently, God did for us. Jesus Christ, God's only Son, left His exalted place with God the Father and humiliated Himself to become a man that He might carry out God's plan of salvation. Jesus Christ, the very Creator and Sustainer of the universe, condescended to become a creature so that He could save those whom God had chosen from before the foundation of the world.

Our previous daily readings merely set the stage for what we are about to examine in the remainder of this book—now we'll see God's plan in action. There's great joy and comfort not only in knowing God chose you to be saved but also in seeing how He accomplished it. That leads us to one of the most profound passages in all Scripture, Philippians 2:5–8 (which we will take three days to explore). Here the apostle Paul described the incarnation of Christ—the central miracle of Christianity:

> Have this attitude in yourselves which was also in Christ Jesus, who, although He existed in the form of God, did not regard equality with God a thing to be grasped, but emptied Himself, taking the form of a bond-servant, and being made in the likeness of men. Being found in appearance as a man, He humbled Himself by becoming obedient to the point of death, even death on a cross. (Phil. 2:5–8)

As crucial as this passage is theologically, it is first and foremost ethical. The context reveals that Paul was striving to motivate believers to live out their faith. Through the inspiration of the Holy Spirit he used the facts of the incarnation to offer the supreme illustration of humility—an illustration we are called to follow. Paul's inspired description is the supreme portrait of self-sacrifice, self-denial, self-giving, and boundless love for God on the part of Christ.

At the same time that we survey His example of humility, we need to see through to His love for us as well. Beyond His example of humility is what that humble act accomplished: the redemption of our souls. Renewing our love for Christ must begin at this point. Only as we remember what He willingly gave up for us will we dutifully follow His example and do nothing out of selfishness or conceit and instead regard others as more important than ourselves. There is no greater way to demonstrate our love for Him.

Paul began by affirming that Jesus is God when he said that He "existed in the form of God" (v. 6). That is the point where the incarnation began and from which Christ began the descent of His humiliation. The Greek word translated "existed" (*huparcho*) stresses the essence of a person's nature—the continuous state or condition of something.[2] It expresses what one is unalterably and inalienably in essence. Paul's point was that Jesus Christ continuously exists without change.

The meaning of the Greek word translated "form" (*morphe*) "always signifies a form which truly and fully expresses the being which underlies it."[3] That means it describes the essential being or nature of that which it refers to, in this case the essential being of God.

Morphe is better understood when compared to the Greek word *schema*, which is also translated "form." *Morphe* expresses the essential character of something—what it is in itself—while *schema* emphasizes outward form or appearance. What *morphe* expresses never changes, while what *schema* represents can. For example, all men possess manhood from the time they are conceived until they die. That is their *morphe*. But the essential character of manhood is shown in various *schema*. At one time a man is an embryo, then a baby, then a child, then a boy, then a youth, then a young man, then an adult, and finally an old man.

By using *morphe* in Philippians 2, Paul was saying Jesus possessed the unchangeable, essential nature of God. That interpretation of the first phrase of verse 6 is strengthened by the second phrase, He "did not regard equality with God a thing to be grasped," which indicates Jesus was equal with God. Being in the form of God thus expresses Christ's equality to God.

The deity of Christ is the heart and soul of the Christian faith. One of the goals of the apostle John in writing his Gospel was to leave his readers with little doubt that Jesus is God. He began by saying:

> In the beginning was the Word [Christ], and the Word was with God, and the Word was God. . . . All things came into being through Him, and apart from Him nothing came into being that has come into being. In Him was life, and the life was the Light of men. (John 1:1, 3–4)

He also said that Christ "became flesh, and dwelt among us, and we saw His glory, glory as of the only begotten from the Father" (v. 14). Earlier, we examined two additional passages that also affirmed the deity of Christ, Colossians 1:15–17 and Hebrews 1:3. Christianity begins with the recognition that Jesus Christ is in essence fully the eternal God. That is also the starting point of Christ's humiliation. He descended from the exalted place of possessing the being of God.

Daily Challenge

Although we cannot begin to understand the humiliation Christ experienced, we can follow His example. After all, we are the children of God, blessed with all spiritual blessings in the heavenlies in Christ (see Eph. 1:3). We have been chosen in Him (see v. 4). We are a special people who have been promised heaven's eternal glory. And we possess an exalted position as sons and daughters of God. Therefore, our humiliation begins with a recognition of the lofty starting point from which we are required to descend for the benefit of others. The simple and profound truth is that God became human and we are to be servants like Him. We are to follow the example of our first love.

Day 9

In the Likeness
of Men

[Christ Jesus] did not regard equality with God a thing to be grasped, but emptied Himself, taking the form of a bond-servant, and being made in the likeness of men.

Philippians 2:6–7

Having gained an appreciation of the supreme height from which Jesus descended, we now see in Paul's teaching the first steps of His noble humiliation in becoming one of us.

Although Jesus was equal with God, He "did not regard equality with God a thing to be grasped." The Greek word translated "equality" (*isos*) describes things exactly equal in size, quantity, quality, character, and number. The first step in Christ's humiliation was His willingness to not hold on to His equality with God. Although He did not cling to it, there is no question that Jesus claimed it and that the people who heard Him knew He claimed it. John wrote, "The Jews were seeking all the more to kill Him, because He not only was breaking the Sabbath, but also was calling God His own Father, making Himself equal with God" (John 5:18). Many today desire to deny the deity of Christ, yet even His worst enemies, the apostate religious leaders, understood full well the significance of His claim: "For a good work we do not stone You, but for blasphemy; and because You, being a man, make Yourself out to be God" (10:33).

Although He possessed all the rights, privileges, and honors of being God, Christ didn't regard them as things "to be grasped." Our Lord proved that loftiness of calling is not something to be held tightly as a prized possession, to be selfishly exploited, or to be never set aside for the benefit of another. Our God looked down on wretched sinners who hated Him and willingly yielded His privileges to give Himself for their sake. The incarnation expresses both the mercy and the unselfish nature of the Second Person of the Trinity.

Instead of clinging to His equality with God, Christ "emptied Himself" (Phil. 2:7). The Greek verb translated "emptied" (*kenoo*) gives us the theological term *kenosis*, which is the doctrine of Christ's self-emptying (a significant aspect of His incarnation). The verb expresses His self-renunciation—His refusal to cling to His advantages and privileges as God as He descended into a humble, human state.

Yet at no time did He empty Himself of His deity in exchange for humanity. He is coexistent with the Father and the Spirit, and for Him to have become less than God would have meant the Trinity would have ceased to exist. Christ could not become less than who He truly is. He retained His divine nature while giving up the following privileges so that He could descend to the desperate level of unworthy sinners.

Shortly before His earthly mission came to a close, Jesus prayed, "Glorify Me together with Yourself, with the glory which I had with You before the world was" (John 17:5). Christ gave up the glory of a face-to-face relationship with God for the muck of this earth. He relinquished the adoring presence of angels for the spittle of men. He sacrificed the shining brilliance of heaven's glories and emptied Himself. On a few occasions during His earthly ministry, the supernatural fullness of the glory of Christ came through, such as on the Mount of Transfiguration (see Luke 9:28–36). You can catch glimpses of Christ's glory in His miracles, attitude, and words, as well as at His crucifixion, His resurrection, and His ascension. But Christ emptied Himself of the continuous outward manifestation and personal enjoyment of heavenly glory.

Our Lord also emptied Himself of His independent authority. He completely submitted Himself to the will of the Father and learned to be a servant. Philippians 2:8 says that He was obedient, and we see that illustrated when He said in the garden, "Not as I will, but as You will" (Matt. 26:39). "He learned obedience from the things which He suffered" (Heb. 5:8) and affirmed that He came to do His Father's will (see John 5:30)—not His own.

Jesus also set aside the prerogatives and expression of His divine nature, voluntarily limiting His divine attributes, though He did not cease being God. For example, He remained omniscient—He "knew what was in man" (2:25). He was still omnipresent—though not physically present, He saw Nathanael under a tree (see 1:45–49). While He didn't give up any of His deity, He did give up the free exercise of His attributes, limiting Himself to the degree of not even knowing the time of His second coming (see Matt. 24:36).

It is impossible for us to fully understand the divine riches that belong to Christ, yet He gave it all up: "Though He was rich, yet for [our] sake He became poor, that [we] through His poverty might become rich" (2 Cor. 8:9). Christ was so poor that He said, "The foxes have holes and the birds of the air have nests, but the Son of Man has nowhere to lay His head" (Matt. 8:20).

God "made Him who knew no sin to be sin on our behalf" (2 Cor. 5:21). As a result, Jesus cried out on the cross, "My God, My God, why have You forsaken Me?" (Matt. 27:46);

He experienced alienation from the Triune God of whom He was part. As He anticipated the completion of His work, He asked the Father to restore that preincarnate glory and relationship (see John 17:4–5).

When Christ emptied Himself, He not only gave up His privileges but He also took "the form of a bond-servant" (Phil. 2:7). Paul again used *morphe* to indicate that Christ took on the essential character of a servant. His servitude was not theatrical or make-believe. He didn't just put on the garment of a slave—He actually became one.

As God, Christ owns everything. But when He came into this world He borrowed everything: a place to be born, a place to sleep, a boat to cross the Sea of Galilee in and preach from, an animal to ride on during His triumphal entry into Jerusalem, a room for the Passover, and a tomb to be buried in. The only person who ever lived on this earth who had the right to everything on it wound up with nothing. That was the incredible destiny of the One of whom it is written, "All things came into being through Him; and apart from Him nothing came into being that has come into being" (John 1:3).

Christ's instruction and example of service for us is clear. After washing the disciples' feet, He said, "If I then, the Lord and the Teacher, washed your feet, you also ought to wash one another's feet. For I gave you an example that you also should do as I did to you" (13:14–15).

Christ's service to sinners took the form of total identification. Paul said that He was "made in the likeness of men" (Phil. 2:7). He was given all the essential attributes of humanity, thus He became like us. He was a genuine human, not just a facsimile. He was more than God in a body—He became the God-man, being fully God and fully man. And like a man, Jesus was born and increased in wisdom and physical maturity (see Luke 2:52).

When Jesus became a man, He took on the nature of man in his fallen and weakened condition: He hurt, He wept, He hungered, He thirsted, He tired, and He died. He was burdened with the results of man's fall.[1] When Christ took on human nature in its fallen character, it was with one significant element eliminated: sin. Jesus was "tempted in all things as we are, yet without sin" (Heb. 4:15).

Daily Challenge

Although Christ never sinned, He felt the results of the fall when He became one of us. Jesus "had to be made like His brethren in all things, so that He might become a merciful and faithful high priest" (Heb. 2:17). As we press on in our journey to know and be conformed to Christ, we can come confidently before Him in prayer, knowing that He completely understands our human weakness.

Day 10
Even Death on a Cross

Being found in appearance as a man, He humbled Himself by becoming obedient to the point of death, even death on a cross.

Philippians 2:8

For God the eternal Son to become one of his own creations and live among us was an astounding act of love. But that alone could never accomplish our salvation. In order to complete God's eternal plan, Jesus had to humble Himself to the level of lowest humanity, and He had to die.

The next step in Christ's descent relates closely to the previous point. Christ was not only "made in the likeness of men"

(Phil. 2:7) but also "found in appearance as a man" (v. 8). The difference between these two phrases is simply a shift in focus. In verse 8 we see the humiliation of Christ from the vantage point of those who saw and experienced Him. Christ was the God-man, but as people looked at Him they saw the appearance (*schema*, the "outward form") of a man. Thus they viewed Him as no different than any other man.

For Christ to become man was humbling enough. For Him not to be recognized as the Messiah must have been even more humbling. He performed miracles and taught authoritatively, yet these were typical responses: "You are a Samaritan and have a demon" (John 8:48) and "Is not this Jesus, the son of Joseph, whose father and mother we know? How does He now say, 'I have come down out of heaven'?" (6:42). Because their minds were darkened by their sin, people recognized His humanity but could not see His deity. They treated the King of kings not only like a man but also like the worst of men—a common criminal.

Instead of fighting back, Christ "humbled Himself" (Phil. 2:8). Consider His trial. Despite unbelievable humiliation, He didn't speak a word in His defense except to agree with His accusers' statements: "You have said it yourself" (Matt. 26:64). They mocked Him, punched Him, pulled out His beard, and treated Him as scum, yet He remained silent and accepted man's abuse through each phase of the trial. He did not demand His rights but rather humbled Himself.

That kind of attitude is certainly lacking in our society. The demand for one's rights echoes throughout the corridors of our courts, the halls of our government, and even from the pews of our churches. What a different example Christ sets. As King, He could have demanded a palace, a chariot, servants, a fine wardrobe, and a kingdom full of jewels. But He lived as a simple man. Just think that the God of the universe stood beside Joseph and helped him in his carpenter's shop in Nazareth!

Christ's humility extended far beyond His poverty and simple way of life. He was willing to die for sinners: "Greater love has no one than this, that one lay down his life for his friends" (John 15:13). Christ volunteered to die—no man took His life from Him (see 10:18). He gave Himself up to an undeserved death.

Christ stooped to die for sinners because that was the way sinful men and women had to be saved. There was no other way to deliver us, since "the wages of sin is death" (Rom. 6:23). God's holiness required that His wrath be satisfied, and that required a sacrifice. For Christ to help sinful people meant that He would have to die in our place and pay the penalty for our sin so that He might lead us out of death and into eternal life.

"Even death on a cross" (Phil. 2:8) calls attention to the most shocking feature of Christ's humiliation. He suffered not just death, but death on a cross—the most excruciating, embarrassing, degrading, painful, and cruel death ever devised.

Crucifixion originated with the Persians and was later adopted by the Romans. They used this method to execute rebellious slaves and the worst of criminals. The Jews hated that form of punishment because "anyone who is hung on a pole is under God's curse" (Deut. 21:23 NIV). Galatians 3:13 says, "Christ redeemed us from the curse of the Law, having become a curse for us—for it is written, 'Cursed is everyone who hangs on a tree.'" The God who created the universe suffered the ultimate human degradation—hanging naked before a mocking world, with nails driven through His hands and feet.

The grace and love of God toward sinners was such that Christ stooped to die for them. At the end of Paul's doctrinal survey of salvation in Romans, he said, "Oh, the depth of the riches both of the wisdom and knowledge of God! How unsearchable are His judgments and unfathomable His ways!" (Rom. 11:33). Paul was in awe of God's plan of salvation—a plan no person would have dreamed to devise.

If we had planned the incarnation, we probably would have designed for Christ to be born in a palace. Of necessity His family would have been wealthy and prominent, and He would have been educated in the finest universities and taught by the most erudite scholars. We would have orchestrated events so that everyone loved, revered, honored, and respected Him. He would have traveled in all the prominent circles and conversed with the most influential people.

We certainly would not have had Him born in a stable to a poor family. He would not have wasted His youth in a carpenter's shop in some obscure town. No ragtag band would have sufficed as His followers—only the elite could have served Him as His disciples.

Ultimately, we would never have allowed Him to be humiliated. We would have imprisoned or executed anyone who spit on Him, mocked Him, or hurt Him. Lest you think you wouldn't have planned it that way, just recall that Peter was prepared to stop the Lord from carrying out the plan of salvation. He rebuked Christ, saying, "God forbid it, Lord! This shall never happen to You" (Matt. 16:22). Yet any plan for the coming of the Messiah that differed from God's would have resulted in the salvation of not one soul. No wonder the psalmist said, "Your judgments are like a great deep" (Ps. 36:6). God's ways are unsearchable, His truths profound. And as deep as God's divine purpose is, it was accomplished in Christ on our behalf.

Benjamin Warfield, the great theologian, offered a fitting conclusion to remind us of what the Lord Jesus Christ did for us:

We see Him among the thousands of Galilee, anointed of God with the Holy Ghost and power, going about doing good: with no pride of birth, though He was a king; with no pride of intellect, though omniscience dwelt within Him; with no pride of power, though all power in heaven and earth was in His hands; or of station, though the fullness of the Godhead dwelt in Him bodily; or of superior goodness or holiness: but in lowliness of mind esteeming every one better than Himself, healing the sick, casting out devils, feeding the hungry, and everywhere breaking to men the bread of life. We see Him everywhere offering to men His life for the salvation of their souls: and when, at last, the forces of evil gathered thick around Him, walking, alike without display and without dismay, the path of suffering appointed for Him, and giving His life at Calvary that through His death the world might live.[1]

 Daily Challenge

Since Christ, the God of the universe, willingly gave up so much for you, what ought you to give up for Him? The least any believer can do is give up what he holds most dear to love and serve the One who can't be anything but most dear and precious to him. Return to the joy of your first love and experience once again the internal joy that comes from knowing you are rightly related to the Lord and Savior.

Day 11
Our Desperate Need

You were dead in your trespasses and sins, in which you formerly walked according to the course of this world, according to the prince of the power of the air, of the spirit that is now working in the sons of disobedience. Among them we too all formerly lived in the lusts of our flesh, indulging the desires of the flesh and of the mind, and were by nature children of wrath, even as the rest.

Ephesians 2:1–3

I was told the story of a great tribal leader known for his fairness and wisdom. One day it was reported that someone in the tribe was stealing. The leader proclaimed that the thief, when captured, would receive ten lashes. But the thievery continued, even as the leader upped the level of punishment eventually to forty lashes, knowing that only a strong man like himself could survive such a severe whipping. The thief was finally apprehended, and to everyone's horror, she turned out to be the leader's own aged mother.

The people speculated what the leader would do. One of his laws required children to love and honor their parents, yet another demanded the public whipping of thieves. Would he satisfy his love and save his mother, or would he satisfy his law and watch his mother die under the whip?

The tribe finally gathered around a large post at the center of the compound. The leader entered and sat on his throne. Then two towering warriors led his frail mother into the compound and tied her to the post. Finally the tribal whip master, a powerful man with bulging muscles, entered carrying a long leather whip. The warriors ripped off the woman's garment, exposing her frail back.

Just then the leader held up his hand to halt the punishment. A sigh of relief went up from the crowd. His love would be satisfied, but what about his law?

The leader strode toward his mother, removing his own shirt. He then wrapped his great arms around his mother, exposing his huge muscular back to the whip master. Breaking the heavy silence, he commanded, "Proceed with the punishment."

That wonderful story illustrates what Christ did for us. As with the leader's mother, our sin put us under the whip of judgment. The apostle Paul warned that "the wages of sin is death" (Rom. 6:23). Sin brings death, inevitably and without exception. After death comes eternal judgment (see Heb. 9:27). Since men are unable to atone for their own sins, God's judgment demands that they pay or have a substitute pay for them.

Left to his own resources, therefore, man has no prospect but death. But God is also loving, and He had a plan to save man from hell—He supplied the Substitute who would satisfy His justice by taking the punishment of man on Himself and dying in his place.

Christ humbled Himself from His exalted throne and came to earth so that He could pay the penalty we owed. Jesus wrapped His arms around us, satisfying His love by enabling us to escape God's wrath and satisfying His law by paying the penalty for our sin.

The substitutionary death of Christ is the essential truth of the Christian faith. Without it there is no gospel, no good news. Commentator Leon Morris wrote:

> To put it bluntly and plainly, if Christ is not my Substitute, I still occupy the place of a condemned sinner. If my sins and my guilt are not transferred to Him, if He did not take them upon Himself, then surely they remain with me. If He did not

deal with my sins, I must face their consequences. If my penalty was not borne by Him, it still hangs over me.[1]

Scripture is filled with reminders of what believers were like prior to their salvation in Christ. Any attempt to reinvigorate our devotion to Christ must begin with a reminder of what He saved us from and the price He had to pay to rescue us.

The apostle Paul stated so simply and profoundly our condition without Christ: "You were dead in your trespasses and sins" (Eph. 2:1; see also Col. 2:13). As we have seen, the wages, or payment, for sin is death (see Rom. 6:23), and because man is born in sin, death is his ultimate future.

Man's basic problem is not lack of harmony with his heritage or environment, as society would have you believe, but his total lack of harmony with his Creator, from whom he is alienated by sin (see Eph. 4:18). He is spiritually dead to all God offers, including righteousness, inner peace, happiness, and ultimately, every good thing. He may go through the motions of life, but he certainly doesn't possess it.

By stating that we were all dead in "trespasses *and* sins," Paul was not describing two different kinds of wrongdoing but simply referring to the breadth of our sinfulness. "Trespasses" refers to stumbling, falling, or going in the wrong direction. The Greek word translated "sins" (*hamartia*) originally meant "to miss the mark," as when a hunter with bow and arrow missed the target. In the spiritual realm it refers to falling short of God's standard of holiness: "All have sinned and fall short of the glory of God" (Rom. 3:23).

Jesus reiterated God's standard when He commanded that we be perfect, just as our Father in heaven is perfect (see Matt. 5:48). God's command to "be holy, for I am holy" (Lev. 11:44; see also 1 Pet. 1:16) did not create a new standard for mankind; He has never had any other standard for man but perfect holiness. No matter how much good man does or attempts to do, the standard of never doing or never having done evil at all is unattainable.

Before salvation, we all used to walk

> according to the course of this world, according to the prince of the power of the air, of the spirit that is now working in the sons of disobedience. Among them we too all formerly lived in the lusts of our flesh, indulging the desires of the flesh and of the mind, and were by nature children of wrath, even as the rest. (Eph. 2:1–3)

We used to think and live according to the world's standards, which are dominated and controlled by Satan.

As a result, "we too all formerly lived in the lusts of our flesh, indulging the desires of the flesh and of the mind" (v. 3). "Lusts" refers to strong desires of every sort, not just sexual lust, while "desires" emphasizes strong willfulness, a seeking after something with great diligence. By nature fallen man is driven to fulfill the lusts and desires of his sinful flesh and mind, completely selfish and abandoned to doing whatever feels good and resolutely defying God.

In writing to the Colossian believers, Paul described their condition as "formerly alienated and hostile in mind, engaged in evil deeds" (Col. 1:21). Before their reconciliation, the Colossians were completely estranged from God because of their sin. Scripture teaches that unbelievers love "the darkness rather than the Light, for their deeds [are] evil. For everyone who does evil hates the Light, and does not come to the Light for fear that his deeds will be exposed" (John 3:19–20). Their problem is not ignorance but willful love of sin.

Sin is the root cause of man's alienation from God. Since God cannot fellowship with sin (see Hab. 1:13; 1 John 1:6), sin must be dealt with before God and man can be reconciled. From God's holy perspective, His just wrath against sin must be appeased.

 Daily Challenge

Apart from gracious reconciliation through Christ, every person by nature is the object of God's wrath—a victim of His eternal condemnation and judgment. Since that is a Christian's former condition, why would any believer

leave the loving relationship he or she has with Christ to pursue again the very thing Christ saved us from? Yet that is what many Christians do today. As you look again at what Christ accomplished on your behalf, I hope you'll be challenged to renew your commitment to love Him above all else.

Day 12
Our Loving Substitute

He Himself bore our sins in His body on the cross, so that we
might die to sin and live to righteousness; for by His wounds
you were healed.

1 Peter 2:24

Before you became a Christian, you stood with every other
unbeliever under God's condemning hand—an enemy with
seemingly no possibility of escape from His judgment. Your
sin declared you guilty before God, and there was no price
you could pay that could cancel your debt to Him. *Hopeless*
would have been the best way to describe your dilemma, and

that's just what Scripture says: "Remember that you were . . . separate from Christ . . . having no hope and without God in the world" (Eph. 2:12).

When you and I were at our most desperate, when nothing we could do could save us, God did. "But God, being rich in mercy, because of His great love with which He loved us, even when we were dead in our transgressions, made us alive together with Christ" (vv. 4–5). Simply because God loved us, He provided a way for us to return to Him. Even though we sinned against Him, through His rich mercy and great love He offered forgiveness and reconciliation to us, just as He does to every repentant sinner.

God loved enough not only to forgive but also to die for the very ones who had offended Him. Paul writes, "For while we were still helpless, at the right time Christ died for the ungodly" (Rom. 5:6). Since we were helpless to bring ourselves to God, He sent His only begotten Son, Jesus Christ, to die for us, notwithstanding the fact that we were ungodly and completely unworthy of His love. When we were powerless to escape from sin and death, helpless against Satan's schemes, and unable to please God in any way, He still sent His Son to die on our behalf. In that one act He proved the wonders of His love. "Greater love has no one than this, that one lay down his life for his friends" (John 15:13). Compassionate love for those who don't deserve it made salvation possible.

Regarding this great love, Paul writes, "God demonstrates His own love toward us, in that while we were yet sinners, Christ died for us" (Rom. 5:8). That sort of selfless, undeserved love is completely beyond our limited, finite comprehension. Yet that is the very love the just and infinitely holy God had toward us even while we were still sinners. When we were still hopelessly enmeshed in our sin, God sent His Son to die in our place.

The apostle Peter says, "He Himself bore our sins in His body on the cross, so that we might die to sin and live to righteousness; for by His wounds you were healed" (1 Pet. 2:24). That description of Christ's death on our behalf is an allusion to Isaiah's description of the substitutionary, sin-bearing death of the Messiah (see Isa. 53:4–5, 11). To emphasize this substitutionary nature of Christ's death, Peter says that He "died for sins once for all, the just for the unjust" (1 Pet. 3:18).

The apostle Paul also emphasized the substitutionary work of Christ. He said that God "made Him who knew no sin to be sin on our behalf, so that we might become the righteousness of God in Him" (2 Cor. 5:21) and that "Christ redeemed us from the curse of the Law, having become a curse for us" (Gal. 3:13).

Some claim it's immoral to teach that God would take on human flesh and bear the sins of men and women in their stead. They say it defies justice to transfer the penalty of sin from a guilty person to an innocent person. But that's not what happened on the cross. Commentator Leon Morris explained what God did:

> When Christ substitutes for sinful man in His death that is God Himself bearing the consequences of our sin, God saving man at cost to Himself, not at cost to someone else. . . . In part the atonement is to be understood as a process whereby God absorbs in Himself the consequences of man's sin.[1]

On the cross Christ willingly took our sin and bore its penalty. Nothing was forced on Him. If He had not willed to take our sin and accept its punishment, as sinners we would have borne the punishment of sin in hell forever. Christ's work on the cross wasn't unfair—it was God's love in action!

First Peter 2:24 says that Christ "Himself bore our sins." "Himself" is emphatic in the text—it was Christ *Himself* who took on sin and bore its penalty. He bore it willingly and voluntarily, and He bore it alone. He indeed was "the Lamb of God who takes away the sin of the world!" (John 1:29).

When Peter said He "bore" our sins, he used a term that means "to carry a massive, heavy weight." That's what sin is. It's so heavy that Romans 8:22 says "the whole creation groans and suffers" under its weight. Only Jesus could remove such a weight from us, and He did so by bearing our sins "in His body on the cross" (1 Pet. 2:24). It was God's plan that Christ be lifted up to die (see John 12:32–33). Paul says that Christ had to be hung on a tree to fulfill the prediction of becoming a curse for us (see Deut. 21:23; Gal. 3:13). So Jesus bore our sins by enduring the wrath of God as He was suspended on a cross of wood.

To better understand just what Christ accomplished for us on that cross, we need to examine the different terms that express the ramifications of Christ's substitutionary death. Several key words describe the richness of our salvation in Christ: *redemption* and its corollary *forgiveness*, *justification*, and *reconciliation*. In redemption, the sinner stands before God as a slave but is granted freedom (see Rom. 6:18–22). In forgiveness, the sinner stands before God as a debtor but the debt is paid and forgotten (see Eph. 1:7). In justification the sinner, though standing before God guilty and condemned, is declared righteous (see Rom. 8:33). In reconciliation, the sinner stands before God as an enemy but becomes His friend (see 2 Cor. 5:18–20). Leon Morris highlighted the importance of those terms in this manner:

> Redemption is substitutionary, for it means that Christ paid the price that we could not pay, paid it in our stead, and we go free. Justification interprets our salvation judicially, and as the New Testament sees it Christ took our legal liability, took it in our stead. Reconciliation means the making of people to be at one by the taking away of the cause of hostility. In this case the cause is sin, and Christ removed that cause for us.

We could not deal with sin. He could and did, and did it in such a way that it is reckoned to us. . . . Was there a price to be paid? He paid it. Was there a victory to be won? He won it. Was there a penalty to be borne? He bore it. Was there a judgment to be faced? He faced it.[2]

Daily Challenge

There's nothing more that can be done on our behalf. How gracious of our Lord to give us this multifaceted understanding of our salvation. We do well to constantly remind ourselves of His amazing and effective grace. Over the next two days we will explore each of these biblical terms in greater depth.

Day 13

Rescued through Redemption

He rescued us from the domain of darkness, and transferred us to the kingdom of His beloved Son, in whom we have redemption, the forgiveness of sins.

Colossians 1:13–14

The passage above is only one of many examples in which Scripture speaks eloquently of our redemption from sin. Paul described redemption as our "having been freed from sin [and becoming] slaves of righteousness" (Rom. 6:18). He also said that Jesus Christ "gave Himself for our sins so that He might rescue us from this present evil age, according to the will of our God and Father" (Gal. 1:4). And he wrote, "In [Christ] we have redemption through His blood, the forgiveness of our trespasses" (Eph. 1:7).

Two Greek legal terms define redemption: *agorazo* and the related *exagorazo* referred to buying or purchasing. In the New Testament they are used to denote spiritual purchase or redemption (see Gal. 3:13; Rev. 5:9). The other term for redemption, *lutroo*, means "to release from captivity." An intensified form, *apolutrosis* (translated "redemption" in Eph. 1:7), was used to refer to paying a ransom to release someone from bondage, especially those under the yoke of slavery.

During New Testament times the Roman Empire had as many as six million slaves, and the buying and selling of them was big business. If someone wanted to free a loved one or friend who was a slave, he would buy him and then grant him his freedom. He would attest to that deliverance with a written certificate. *Lutroo* was used to designate such a transaction.

That is precisely the idea expressed in the New Testament use of the term to represent Christ's atoning sacrifice on the cross. Picture sin as man's captor and slave owner, demanding a price for his release, with death as the price. Biblical redemption is the act by which God Himself pays the ransom price to satisfy His own holy justice and to buy back fallen men and women and set them free from their sin.

Jesus Christ is our Redeemer from sin. He paid the price for our release from iniquity and death. Because we now belong to Christ and by faith are made one with Him, we are now acceptable to God. Every Christian is God's beloved child because the Lord Jesus Christ has become our Redeemer. The Hebrew concept of a kinsman-redeemer (see Ruth) set forth three qualifications: the redeemer had to (1) be related to the one needing redemption, (2) be able to pay the price, and (3) be willing to do so. The Lord Jesus Christ perfectly met those requirements.

Those receiving redemption are the "we" of Ephesians 1:7—"the saints . . . who are faithful in Christ Jesus" (v. 1). Based on our earlier discussion, we are acutely aware of our need for redemption. We were once sinners and desperate for a Redeemer. We can thank God that Christ "gave Himself for us to redeem us from every lawless deed, and to purify for Himself a people for His own possession, zealous for good deeds" (Titus 2:14).

The price of our redemption is "His blood" (Eph. 1:7). It cost the blood of the Son of God to buy men back from the slave market of sin. Shedding of blood is a term not limited to the fluid but also a metonym for Christ's violent death on the cross. Scripture shows us that Christ gave not only His blood (see Acts 20:28) but also His very life (see Matt. 20:28) and self (see Gal. 1:4). Through the sacrifice of His Son, God showed us mercy without violating His justice. Through His bloody death, our Lord poured out His life as a sacrificial, substitutionary payment for sin. That which we deserved and could not save ourselves from, the beloved Savior, though He did not deserve it, took upon Himself. He made payment for what otherwise would have condemned us to death and hell.

We "were not redeemed with perishable things like silver or gold . . . but with precious blood, as of a lamb unblemished and spotless, the blood of Christ" (1 Pet. 1:18–19). No human, earthly commodity like silver or gold suffices to redeem man. No one can purchase redemption from sin by the payment of any perishable commodity.

But "the precious blood" of Christ could. Peter here compares the preciousness of Christ's death to that of an unblemished, spotless lamb—the finest, purest lamb any shepherd could own and the ultimate sacrifice any shepherd could make. Christ was the ultimate sacrifice of God, sufficient to redeem us from our bondage to sin. Christ was "the Lamb of God who takes away the sin of the world!" (John 1:29). The precious blood of Christ—emblematic of His sacrificial, substitutionary death—frees us from the guilt, condemnation, power, and penalty of sin and ultimately one glorious day will remove us from the presence of sin.

The marvelous result of redemption for the believer is complete forgiveness of all sin. Speaking to the disciples about the Lord's Supper, Christ said, "This is My blood of the covenant, which is poured out for many for forgiveness of sins" (Matt. 26:28). Redemption brings forgiveness, because "without shedding of blood there is no forgiveness" (Heb. 9:22).

The Greek word often translated "forgiveness" (*aphiemi*) means "to send away never to return." Used as a legal term, it meant to repay or cancel a debt or to grant a pardon. Through the shedding of His own blood, Jesus Christ actually took the sins of the world upon His own head, as it were, and carried them an infinite distance away, from where they could never return.

To illustrate how permanent our forgiveness in Christ is, Paul wrote the Colossians saying that when God forgave us, He "canceled out the certificate of debt consisting of decrees against us, which was hostile to us; and He has taken it out of the way, having nailed it to the cross" (Col. 2:14). "Certificate of debt" referred to a document handwritten by the debtor in acknowledgment of his debt.

Paul described that certificate as "consisting of decrees against us." All people owe God a debt because they have violated His law. The certificate was "hostile to us" in that it was enough to condemn us to judgment and hell. But God canceled it out and wiped it away, like you would erase chalk from a blackboard. In that day, documents were commonly written either on papyrus, a paperlike material made from the bulrush plant, or vellum, which was made from an animal's hide. The ink they used contained no acid, thus it didn't soak into the material and could easily be wiped off if the scribe wanted to reuse the material. In a similar way, God has wiped off our certificate of debt, "having nailed it to the cross." Not a trace of it remains to be held against us.

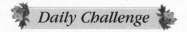

Daily Challenge

It is so tragic when so many Christians get depressed about their faults and failures, thinking and acting as if God still holds their sins against them. They have forgotten that since God has placed their sins upon Himself, they are separated from those sins "as far as the east is from the west" (Ps. 103:12). Before He even made the earth, He placed the sins of His elect on His Son, who took them an eternal distance away. He dismissed our sins before we were born, and they can never return. "Therefore there is now no condemnation for those who are in Christ Jesus. For the law of the Spirit of life in Christ Jesus has set you free from the law of sin and of death" (Rom. 8:1–2). I hope today that you'll take to heart the fact that while forgiveness in Jesus Christ is undeserved, it is free and complete, and it is entirely "according to the riches of His grace which He lavished on us" (Eph. 1:7–8).

Day 14

Righteous through Justification

Therefore, having been justified by faith, we have peace with God through our Lord Jesus Christ.

Romans 5:1

From redemption and forgiveness we move to *justification*—the term that describes the judicial verdict of God on behalf of the redeemed sinner. The Greek word *dikaioo* and its related terms referred to legal acquittal of a charge and are used theologically to speak of a sinner being vindicated, justified, and declared righteous before God.

Justification is God's declaration that all the demands of the law are fulfilled on behalf of the believing sinner through the righteousness of Jesus Christ. As a wholly forensic or legal transaction, justification changes the judicial *standing* of the sinner before God. In justification, God *imputes* the perfect righteousness of Christ to the believer's account, then declares the redeemed one fully righteous. Christ's own infinite merit is the ground on which the believer stands before God. Paul said that we have been "justified by His blood" (Rom. 5:9). Thus justification raises us to a level of complete acceptance and divine privilege in Christ. As a result, believers are not only perfectly free from any charge of guilt (see 8:33) but also have the full merit of Christ reckoned to their personal account (see 5:17). It is important to note, however, the distinction between justification and sanctification. In sanctification God actually *imparts* Christ's righteousness to the sinner.

While the two must be distinguished, justification and sanctification can never be separated. God does not justify whom He does not sanctify.[1]

The most immediate consequence of our justification is our reconciliation, which brings us peace with God. The Greek legal term translated "reconcile" (*katallasso*) meant to bring together two disputing parties. In the New Testament it is used to speak of a believer's reconciliation to God through Jesus Christ.

Because most unbelievers have no conscious hatred of God and don't actively oppose Him, they don't consider themselves to be His enemies. But the fact is that the mind of every unsaved person is self-centered and at peace only with the things of the flesh, and therefore by definition is "hostile toward God" (8:7). God is the enemy of the sinner, and that enmity cannot end unless and until the sinner places his or her trust in Jesus Christ.

Once a person embraces Christ in repentant faith, the sinless Son of God, who made perfect satisfaction for all our sins (an element of Christ's work that we'll examine on a later day), makes that person eternally at peace with God the Father. Beyond that "He Himself is our peace" (Eph. 2:14).

Full reconciliation with God is ours through the Lord Jesus. Because He possesses all the fullness of deity (see Col. 1:19), He is able to fully reconcile sinful men and women to God, "having made peace through the blood of His cross . . . He has now reconciled you in His fleshly body through death" (vv. 20, 22). Only His violent death on the cross could effect our reconciliation with God. Those who trust in Christ are no longer God's enemies or under His wrath but rather are at peace with Him.

Perhaps no passage stresses the vital importance of reconciliation more than 2 Corinthians 5:17–21, in which we can discern five truths. First, reconciliation transforms men: "If anyone is in Christ, he is a new creature; the old things passed away; behold, new things have come" (v. 17). Second, it appeases God's wrath: "He made Him who knew no sin to be sin on our behalf, so that we might become the righteousness of God in Him" (v. 21). Third, it comes through Christ: "All these things are from God, who reconciled us to Himself through Christ" (v. 18). Fourth, it is available to all who believe: "God was in Christ reconciling the world to Himself" (v. 19). Finally, every believer has been given the ministry of proclaiming the message of reconciliation: God "gave us the ministry of reconciliation" and "He has committed to us the word of reconciliation" (vv. 18, 19).

God sends His people forth as ambassadors into a fallen, lost world, bearing amazing good news. People everywhere are hopelessly lost and doomed, cut off from God by sin. But God has provided the means of reconciliation through the death of His Son. Our mission is to plead with people to receive that reconciliation before it is too late. Paul's attitude should be true of every believer: "Therefore, we are ambassadors for Christ, as though God were making an appeal through us; we beg you on behalf of Christ, be reconciled to God" (v. 20).

To be ambassadors, we must be able to live the part. And that was God's ultimate goal in effecting our redemption, justification, and reconciliation. We just looked at 2 Corinthians 5:21, where Paul said, "He made Him who knew no sin to be sin on our behalf, that we might become the righteousness of God in Him." In Colossians 1:22 Paul said the goal of reconciliation is "to present you before Him holy and blameless and beyond reproach." And Peter said, "He Himself bore our sins in His body on the cross, so that we might die to sin and live to righteousness" (1 Pet. 2:24). Those verses don't claim that Christ died so we could go to heaven, have peace, or experience love; He died to bring about a transformation—to make saints out of sinners.

The Greek word translated "die" (*apoginomai*) in 1 Peter 2:24 is used only here in the New Testament. It means to "depart" or "cease existing." Christ's substitutionary work enables a person to depart from a life of sin and enter into an eternally new life pattern: a life of righteousness.

The apostle Paul said, "Our old self was crucified with [Christ], in order that our body of sin might be done away with, so that we would no longer be slaves to sin" (Rom. 6:6). Our identification with Christ in His death results in our walking "in newness of life" (v. 4). We have died to sin, thus it no longer has a claim on us. First Peter 2:24 echoes that thought: our identification with Christ in His death is a departure from sin and a new direction in life.

Let's review the last few days: we began life as enemies of God, guilty of violating His standard of holiness, living a life of slavery to sin, and owing God a debt we could never repay.

But through Christ, God bathed us in His love, offering up His Son as the ransom price in payment of our sin and thus accomplishing our redemption, forgiveness, justification, and reconciliation.

Daily Challenge

If God so loved us, how can we not love Him and His Son with the depth of our whole being? What Christ accomplished for us deserves our utmost devotion. Anything less than undying love to Him depreciates His wondrous work on the cross. It is my sincere prayer that by continually remembering what you once were without Christ, and by realizing what you have now that you are in Him, you will revitalize your love for Him.

Day 15
Inadequate Sacrifices

You were not redeemed with perishable things like silver or gold from your futile way of life inherited from your forefathers, but with precious blood, as of a lamb unblemished and spotless, the blood of Christ.

1 Peter 1:18–19

In a small village somewhere in England there once stood a chapel, and over the arch beside it were written the words, "We Preach Christ Crucified." For years godly men preached there, presenting a crucified Savior as the only means of salvation.

As that generation of godly preachers passed on, there arose a different generation who considered the cross and its message to be too antiquated. So they began preaching salvation by Christ's example rather than by His blood, ignoring the necessity of His sacrifice. Meanwhile, ivy had crept up the side of the arch and covered the word *crucified*, and the arch now read, "We Preach Christ." And they did preach Him, but not as having been crucified.

Eventually people in the congregation began to question the practice of confining sermons to Christ and the Bible. So the preachers began to give discourses on such topics as social issues, politics, philosophy, and moral rearmament. The ivy continued to grow until it wiped out the third word, rendering the phrase simply, "We Preach."

The apostle Paul wrote to the cultured Corinthians, saying, "I determined to know nothing among you except Jesus Christ, and Him crucified" (1 Cor. 2:2). The only hope of men is indeed Christ crucified, and that is the theme of Hebrews 10:1–18, the primary passage we will examine over the next three days. Previously we analyzed Christ's substitutionary death on the cross and what it accomplished from a legal standpoint. We learned that salvation from judgment demands the substitution of a death. Over the next three days we'll see that Jesus's sacrifice was superior to any offered in the Old Testament system. His death became the great and final sacrifice that accomplished for eternity what all the other sacrifices couldn't.

Christians today can easily become complacent in their love of Christ when they are continually exposed to a society that is only too eager to tolerate and excuse any sin. When churches reinforce that attitude by their own unwillingness to expose and deal with sin in either their congregation or leadership, believers will stagnate in their zeal for Christ. Why should they work hard at building their relationship with Him when they sense no urgent need to do so?

In stark contrast, the people who lived under the old covenant were continually exposed to a religious system that exacerbated their lack of a vital, dynamic relationship with the living God. To understand how crucial Christ's sacrifice was for you and what it accomplished, you need to first gain some insight into what it was like to live under the Mosaic law.

Under the old covenant, the priests remained busy from dawn to sunset slaughtering and sacrificing animals. Particularly at Passover, many thousands were slain in a week. But no matter how many sacrifices were made, or how often, they were ineffective both individually and collectively. They failed in three ways: (1) they were unable to give anyone access to God, (2) they could not remove sin, and (3) they were only external.

The great cry in the hearts of the Old Testament saints was to be in the presence of God (see Exod. 33:15). Yet all the old ceremonies and sacrifices, though offered continually, could never save, never "make perfect those who draw near" (Heb. 10:1).

That's because the law was only "a shadow of the good things to come and not the very form" (v. 1). The law and its ceremonies could only reflect the very form of the good things to come: the privileges and blessings that would result from the sacrifice of Christ. They were form without substance. Christ's sacrifice, however, is the "very form" (*eikon*)—the exact replica or reproduction of "the good things to come." He brought forgiveness, peace, a clear conscience, and most significantly, access to God.

The good things foreshadowed and implied in the old system came to pass in Christ. The purpose of the law was never "to make perfect"—to bring to completion the salvation people desired. But God did have some important goals for the law: (1) as a shadow, it pointed the people toward the coming reality of salvation (see 1 Pet. 1:10), (2) it served as a reminder that the penalty of sin is death, and (3) God gave His people the sacrifices as a covering for sin. When properly offered from a true heart of faith, the old sacrifices removed immediate, temporal judgment from God. To despise the sacrifices was to be "cut off from among his people" (Lev. 17:4) and incur God's temporal punishment. So the sacrifices, while unable to bring a person into God's presence, were important in maintaining a demonstration of a person's covenantal relationship to Him.

The people who lived under Mosaic law sought deliverance from the sin and accompanying guilt that ate away at their consciences. But their sacrifices couldn't deliver them from sin. In fact, the sacrifices served as a constant reminder that they couldn't escape it. That's what the writer of Hebrews pointed out: "Would they not have ceased to be offered, because the worshipers, having once been cleansed, would no longer have had consciousness of sins? But in those sacrifices there is a reminder of sins year by year" (Heb. 10:2–3).

If the sacrifices had really done their job in removing sin, the people wouldn't have been burdened by its guilt. Their consciences were never cleansed as in Christ (see 9:9, 14). If at any time the sacrificial system actually removed their guilt and brought them into fellowship with God, it would have ceased to be necessary because it would have accomplished its perfect end. But it never did—it just reminded them that it was ineffective for removing sin.

Imagine how burdensome living under a system like that must have been. Instead of being able to offer the sacrifice and reap forgiveness, they were constantly aware that their next sin required yet another sacrifice, which in turn was powerless to remove the sin or to purify and free their consciences from the guilt of that sin. In fact, the more faithful and godly the person, the guiltier he was likely to feel, because he was more aware of and sensitive to God's holiness and his own sinfulness. He was torn between his knowledge of God's law and his awareness of his own breaking of that law.

While sin is manifested outwardly, its root is always internal. That is an unreachable area for the old sacrifices—they could not go inside a person and change him: "It is impossible for the blood of bulls and goats to take away sins" (Heb. 10:4). Hebrews 9:13–14 clarifies for us what was necessary to transform men: "If the blood of goats and bulls and the ashes of a heifer sprinkling those who have been defiled sanctify for the cleansing of the flesh, how much more will the blood of Christ, who through the eternal Spirit offered Himself without blemish to God, cleanse your conscience from dead works to serve the living God?"

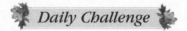

Daily Challenge

There was no real relationship between the death of an animal and the forgiveness of a person's moral offense against God. It was impossible for any animal to satisfy the demands of the holy God. Only Jesus Christ, the perfect union of humanity and deity, could satisfy God and purify humanity. Only His death could be the ultimate, effective sacrifice. Living in that truth enables us to be truly free of guilt as we draw closer to our perfect, and perfectly holy, Savior.

Day 16
The Perfect Sacrifice

By this will we have been sanctified through the offering of the body of Jesus Christ once for all. . . . He, having offered one sacrifice for sins for all time, sat down at the right hand of God.

Hebrews 10:10, 12

Humans in every culture throughout history have contrived methods for denying, ignoring, or attempting to remedy our fundamental problem: sin. Sacrifice is a common historic theme, whether expressed through the shedding of animal or human blood or through the forfeit of wealth, time, or other resources in philanthropic generosity. But none of these efforts ever removed a single sin from a single tarnished soul. Only the sacrifice provided by God Himself can bestow on us the true righteousness we need.

Christ's unique sacrifice was effective for several reasons, which we will examine over the next two days.

As we noted earlier, in eternity past God the Father made a covenant with God the Son in which He would give the Son a unique gift in the form of a redeemed humanity, who would forever praise and glorify Him. To effect this promise, however, God could redeem fallen humanity only by sending His Son to earth to die. Christ's part in God's plan was to be the sacrifice that would accomplish atonement for sin. Hebrews 10:5 says, "When He comes into the world, He says, 'Sacrifice and offering You have not desired, but a body You have prepared for Me.'" When Christ was ready to be incarnated, He acknowledged the inadequacy of the old system and that His own body was to be the sacrifice that would please God and redeem all sinners who were part of the covenant.

On the cross Christ ratified the eternal covenant. He did that which was necessary to provide the redemption the Father had planned from before the foundation of the world.

No matter what the Father asked of Him, Christ was always prepared to accomplish His Father's will. In response to the Father's plan, He said, "I have come (in the scroll of the book it is written of Me) to do Your will, O God" (v. 7). Christ became the perfect sacrifice because He offered Himself in perfect obedience, thus fulfilling God's ultimate will.

The sacrifice of Jesus Christ eliminated the old system and replaced it with a new one. "After saying above, 'Sacrifices and offerings and whole burnt offerings and sacrifices for sin You have not desired, nor have You taken pleasure in them,' (which are offered according to the Law), then He said, 'Behold, I have come to do Your will.' He takes away the first in order to establish the second" (vv. 8–9). The writer's point was to show his Jewish readers that the old covenant was not, never had been, and never would be satisfactory. He sees God's displeasure with the old and His preparation of Christ as evidence that He planned to take "away the first, that He may establish the second." God's focus all along was always on the second covenant. Whatever purpose and validity the first one had God had now set aside.

We've already seen that the old system could not make anyone holy, so God had to establish a system that could. "By this will we have been sanctified through the offering of the body of Jesus Christ once for all" (v. 10). To be sanctified, or made holy, basically means to be set apart from sin. In the context of this verse it refers to salvation.

The construction of the words "we are sanctified" in the Greek text is a perfect participle with a finite verb, showing in the strongest way the permanent and continuous state of salvation in which the believer exists. That means each believer has been permanently made holy. One act, in one moment, provided permanent sanctification for everyone who places his or her trust in Christ.

On the cross He sanctified us and set us apart unto Himself.

Our experience, however, teaches us a different reality. It is difficult to think of ourselves as holy because we constantly are having to deal with sin. In thought and practice we are far from holy, but in the new nature we are perfectly holy. "In Him [we] have been made complete" (Col. 2:10). We may not always act holy, but we are holy in standing before God, just as a child who does not obey his father remains his father's child.

We are holy in the sense that before God the righteousness of Christ has been applied and imputed on our behalf. Our holiness is an accomplished fact—we have been sanctified. Regardless of how holy our walk may be, in our *standing* we are completely and permanently set apart unto God if we have trusted in "the offering of the body of Jesus Christ once for all" (Heb. 10:10).

What the other covenant couldn't do—remove sin—the new covenant in Christ can. "Every priest stands daily ministering and offering time after time the same sacrifices, which can never take away sins; but He, having offered one sacrifice for sins for all time, sat down at the right hand of God" (vv. 11–12).

The Levitical priesthood consisted of twenty-four orders, and in each of those orders hundreds of priests took turns serving at the altar. According to verse 11, the priests always stood while offering the sacrifices because their work was never complete. And their service of these continual sacrifices occupied them daily. In spite of their numbers and their ongoing efforts, not one of them could make an effective sacrifice for sin.

You would assume that if any member of the priesthood could make an effective offering for sin, the high priest could. Once each year, on the Day of Atonement, he would enter the Holy of Holies to make a sacrifice on behalf of his people. On that occasion he would sprinkle blood on the mercy seat, symbolizing the payment of the penalty for his own sins and the sins of the people. But that yearly act, although divinely prescribed and honored, had no power to remove or pay the penalty for a single sin. It could only point to the "merciful and faithful high priest" who would "make propitiation for the sins of the people" (2:17).

"Propitiation" carries the basic idea of appeasement or satisfaction. Jesus Christ was the one Priest whose sacrifice was perfectly and permanently effective in appeasing the wrath of God because He paid the penalty for sin "by the sacrifice of Himself" (9:26). He was "offered once to bear the sins of many" (v. 28). He then "sat down at the right hand of God" (10:12) because He completed His sacrifice, having removed the sins of believers for all time.

Daily Challenge

Some things can never be reproduced, and the sacrifice of Christ is certainly one of them. It's possible, for example, to reproduce poor art, or even poor music. But if someone were to ask you to duplicate a Rembrandt, write a symphony like Beethoven or a fugue like Bach, or to write blank verse like Shakespeare or the hexameters of Homer's Iliad, you couldn't do it. They are masterpieces, and as such stand alone—and those are just examples from the human realm. Beyond those examples, the sacrifice of Christ is the masterpiece of the ages. It cannot be reproduced or repeated, nor should it be, for it removed sins once for all on behalf of those who believe. We have the amazing privilege of living in that reality as we gaze upon the wonder of wonders: the cross of Jesus Christ.

Day 17
The One Eternal Sacrifice

For by one offering He has perfected for all time those who are sanctified. . . . Now where there is forgiveness of these things, there is no longer any offering for sin.

Hebrews 10:14, 18

When Jesus, the Son of God, sacrificed Himself on the cross, He perfectly fulfilled the Trinity's plan. Here was the divine Lamb, foreshadowed by every sacrificial animal under the Old Testament system. His costly gift alone brought salvation, completely removing sin and guilt from those who would receive Him.

Astounding though all of that is, Jesus accomplished even more when He surrendered His life for us. His one sacrifice effected eternal changes on both the earthly and heavenly planes.

All the sacrifices of the Old Testament were unable to deal with Satan. They had absolutely no effect on him at all, nor on the demons and godless men who served him. But when Jesus died on the cross, He dealt a deathblow to all His enemies. First, the cross guaranteed the ultimate destruction of "him who had the power of death, that is, the devil" (Heb. 2:14). The only way to destroy Satan was to rob him of his weapon, which was death—physical, spiritual, and eternal death. And Christ did so through His own death and His ultimate resurrection, thus proving He had conquered death.

In addition to dealing with Satan, Christ also triumphed over all the other fallen angels, and He disarmed and triumphed over all rulers and authorities of all ages who have rejected and opposed God (see Col. 2:14–15). He is now only waiting until all "His enemies be made a footstool" (Heb. 10:13)—until they acknowledge His lordship by bowing at His feet (see Phil. 2:10).

All the enemies of God throughout all the ages gathered their strength together, and the best they could do was cause His physical death on a cross. Yet it was on that very cross that Christ won the victory over them. Their instrument of death became Christ's symbol of triumph over death. He conquered death for all who ever have believed and ever will believe in God. Jesus Christ turned Satan's worst into God's best.

The author of Hebrews said, "By one offering He has perfected for all time those who are sanctified" (10:14). By one offering Christ brought us into God's presence forever. Consistent with the context of the verse, "perfected" refers to our eternal salvation. We can be secure in the fact that His death removes sin forever for those who belong to Him.

Of course, we need continual cleansing when we fall into sin, but we need never fear that our sin will bring about God's judgment on us. As far as Christ's sacrifice is concerned, it sufficed to sanctify and perfect us permanently and provide ongoing forgiveness. That's why He had to sacrifice Himself only once. The writer of Hebrews clarified this truth for us when he said, "Where there is forgiveness of these things, there is no longer any offering for sin" (v. 18).

God had promised to bring about a new covenant, and when Jesus died, that new covenant was sealed with His blood. By quoting the prophecy of the new covenant from Jeremiah 31:33–34, the writer of Hebrews clearly revealed God's intention: "The Holy Spirit also testifies to us; for after saying, 'This is the covenant that I will make with them after those days, says the Lord: I will put My laws upon their heart, and on their mind I will write them,' He then says, 'And their sins and their lawless deeds I will remember no more'" (10:15–17). Jeremiah prophesied that the new covenant would deal with man internally, making it possible for sin to be forgiven and washed away. The new sacrifice was effective. It had to accomplish the things God had promised, because His promises can never be broken.

The writer concluded by saying, "Where there is forgiveness of these things, there is no longer any offering for sin" (v. 18). The work of sacrifice is finished. Forgiveness is already provided for those who trust in Christ's one perfect sacrifice. We can be thankful that we live on this side of the cross, in the glories of that perfect sacrifice, not needing to look forward to something we cannot quite see but able to look back to that which is crystal clear.

How wonderful it is to know that there is no condemnation for those who are in Christ (see Rom. 8:1). It is a wonderful thing to be free from guilt and to recognize that our sins are continually being forgiven by the grace of God through the death of Christ. Our consciences are cleansed!

That's not to say the believer is not aware of or sensitive to his own sin. No one should be more aware of it than the Christian, because, just as the faithful and godly Old Testament saint, he is more aware of God's holiness and standard of righteousness. So while he should be aware of his sin, he need not be unduly burdened with it. The forgiven sinner knows he is forgiven in Christ and is thereby delivered from fear of judgment. This is why true Christians can live in peace, joy, and unconditional love.

Theologian Benjamin B. Warfield appropriately summed up what the sacrifice of Christ means for Christianity:

> Not only is the doctrine of the sacrificial death of Christ embodied in Christianity as an essential element of the system, but in a very real sense it constitutes Christianity. It is this which differentiates Christianity from other religions. Christianity did not come into the world to proclaim a new morality and, sweeping away all the supernatural props by which men were wont to support their trembling, guilt-stricken souls, to throw them back on their own strong right arms to conquer a standing before God for themselves. It came to proclaim the real sacrifice for sin which God had provided in order to supersede all the poor fumbling efforts which men had made and were making to provide a sacrifice for sin for themselves; and, planting men's feet on this, to bid them go forward. It was in this sign that Christianity conquered, and it is in this sign alone that it continues to conquer.[1]

 Daily Challenge

In summary, let me remind you of what Christ has done for you: the God and Sustainer of the universe

humiliated Himself to become a man, suffered by hanging on a cross, and satisfied God's justice by taking man's punishment on Himself, dying in his place, and offering Himself as the one, final, perfect sacrifice. How can you ignore your relationship with the One who did all that for you? Yet many of you do whenever you give someone or something a higher priority in your life. Don't let that happen—give Him first place in your life and learn to view everything from His perspective.

Day 18
The Name above All Names

For this reason also, God highly exalted Him, and bestowed on Him the name which is above every name.

Philippians 2:9

Much as a drowning man searches for a hand that will grasp his and pull him to safety, man longs for eternal life. That illustration was made real to me when Tom, a man who serves in ministry with me, related the story of his own near drowning. When he was a high school senior, Tom and several friends from his church group went swimming in the Blackwater River in Florida. Rain had fallen earlier in the day, and as a result, the river was higher than normal and was running swiftly.

After several minutes of play in the river, Tom realized his legs were very tired, almost as if they were weighed down with lead. The fact that he was wearing jeans didn't help. Since he was unable to continue treading water, he sank like a rock to the bottom, which was about eight to ten feet down. As soon as he reached the riverbed, he pushed off against it and rose back up to the surface. He called out to his friend nearest him on the shore. As the current carried him farther downstream, Tom sank again. He pushed off the bottom once again, but this time he was barely able to break the surface.

Tom went under a third time. When he pushed off the bottom this time, he realized he was not going to make it to the surface. As he rose to within a few inches, he saw through the shimmering water the outline of a hand stretching out toward him. He reached for that hand and managed to grab it! Immediately he flexed all the muscles in his arm and, with the strength of his friend, was pulled out of the water.

Tom was fortunate—his friend happened to be in the right position and had the power to save him. Apart from him, Tom would have drowned that day. When it comes to spiritual rescue from judgment and hell, our Savior was able and eager to reach out to us and save us from eternal death. He assures us, "Because I live, you will live also" (John 14:19).

Our risen Lord and Savior has given His brethren (those who trust and believe in His ability to save them) the greatest gift of all—eternal *life*. How any believer, then, could neglect or ignore his or her relationship to Christ is beyond comprehension. Yet many Christians do, allowing their self-centeredness and the enticements of the world to distract and dominate their thinking so that they turn from looking to Christ, leaving their first love. All believers would do well—both those who need to return to their first love and those who still love Him with the devotion of their heart, soul, mind, and strength—to recall how God rewarded His Son because of His willingness to die for sinners.

In the previous daily readings we considered the humiliation of Christ—how He fulfilled God's plan to save man.

> Although He existed in the form of God, [He] did not regard equality with God a thing to be grasped, but emptied Himself, taking the form of a bond-servant, and being made in the likeness of men. Being found in appearance as a man, He humbled Himself by becoming obedient to the point of death, even death on a cross. (Phil. 2:6–8)

In so doing, Jesus became the perfect substitute and sacrifice—He died in our place, took our sins on His sinless frame, and reconciled us to God by appeasing God's wrath.

Yet if Christ's work on the cross ended with His death and was a noble martyrdom only, we would be drowning men and women, with no one nearby to reach out to pull us to safety. However sacrificial His death was, a dead Savior couldn't deliver sinners because that would mean He was unable to conquer the penalty of sin—death. But Jesus Christ did defeat death and rose again.

> For this reason also, God highly exalted Him, and bestowed on Him the name which is above every name, so that at the name of Jesus every knee will bow, of those who are in heaven and on earth and under the earth, and that every tongue will confess that Jesus Christ is Lord, to the glory of God the Father. (vv. 9–11)

So then, the gospel is not complete without the exaltation of Jesus Christ. In this text, which is likely a hymn of the early church, we see our Lord descending from His glory as God to take on the form of a servant, dying, rising, and then ascending and returning to the glory He had with the Father before the world began. That is the complete Christian message. The humiliation and death of Jesus was only the first phase.

Over the next several days we'll look at the next stage in the unfolding of God's plan for the incarnate Lord and discover how our Savior regained the glory He had with the Father before the world existed (see John 17:5). In Philippians 2:9–11, Paul didn't treat God's exaltation of Christ in the same step-by-step manner that he used in verses 6–8 to describe His descent to become a man. But Scripture as a whole attests to several steps that do comprise and complete His exaltation: His resurrection, ascension, coronation, and present intercession. These are the steps we'll explore in greater detail in the next five daily devotionals.

And overarching this entire sequence, Paul highlights Jesus's triumphant acquisition of a new name.

According to Philippians 2:9, when "God highly exalted Him, [He] bestowed on Him the name which is above every name." We have to ask, then, what is *the* name that is above every name? Hebrews 1:4 says this name is more excellent than the angels' names. It has to be a name that goes beyond merely distinguishing one person from another; it must be a name that is descriptive of Christ's nature—revealing something of His essential being. It has to be a superlative name—one that would set Christ beyond all others and above all comparison.

The only name mentioned in Philippians 2:9–11 that could satisfy such requirements is "Lord." In verse 11 Paul says, "Every tongue will confess that Jesus Christ is Lord." "Lord" is the name that is above every name, because whoever is Lord is the supreme one. "Jesus" is His name of humiliation. "Christ" is His title. "Lord" is His name of exaltation.

Christ acknowledged before Pilate that He was a King (see Mark 15:2; John 18:37). Thomas looked on the resurrected Christ and it was always evident that Christ was the living God and thus Lord; it was in His exaltation that He was formally given the name "Lord," the name above every name.

The Greek word translated "Lord" (*kurios*) primarily refers to the right to rule, thus its inherent meaning is not deity but rulership. *Kurios* was used in the New Testament to describe a master or owner. It was a title of respect for anyone in control and became the official title of the Roman emperors. To say Jesus is *kurios* certainly implies deity, but sovereign authority is the main idea. Regardless of the word's exact meaning, all must acknowledge Jesus's supremacy and right to rule.

We cannot know Christ any other way than as Lord. That's why the first creed in the history of the church, given in Philippians 2:11, says, "Jesus Christ is Lord." Paul said, "We do not preach ourselves but Christ Jesus as Lord" (2 Cor. 4:5). Salvation comes only to those who confess Jesus as Lord (see Rom. 10:9–10). Every Christian must acknowledge that—it's the very substance of Christianity. Jesus is Lord and those who refuse Him as Lord cannot call Him Savior. Everyone who truly receives Him is divinely brought to surrender to His authority.

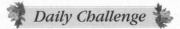

Daily Challenge

As sovereign Lord, Jesus commands and deserves our allegiance and love. Nothing less will suffice. If you call yourself a Christian, your love to Him must be your ultimate priority. "If you love Me," He said, "you will keep My commandments" (John 14:15). Obedience from the heart is the evidence of first love. It is my sincere hope that in seeing your exalted Lord, you will realize how much He deserves your complete and undivided love and loyalty.

Day 19
Our Risen Lord

God raised Him up again, putting an end to the agony of
death, since it was impossible for Him to be held in its power.

Acts 2:24

The resurrection of Jesus Christ is without question the pin-
nacle of redemptive history. It proves beyond a doubt the deity
of Jesus Christ and guarantees our own resurrection. Most
important, it is the crowning proof that God accepted the
sacrifice of Jesus Christ, "who was delivered over because of
our transgressions, and was raised because of our justification"
(Rom. 4:25). Paul's imagery in that verse pictures a criminal
being remanded to his punishment. In a similar manner Jesus

Christ was delivered up as our substitute to serve the sentence of death our transgressions deserved. But He was also raised up to provide the justification before God we could never attain on our own. The great nineteenth-century theologian Charles Hodge wrote:

> With a dead Saviour, a Saviour over whom death had triumphed and held captive, our justification had been forever impossible. As it was necessary that the high priest, under the old economy, should not only slay the victim at the altar, but carry the blood into the most holy place, and sprinkle it upon the mercy-seat; so it was necessary not only that our great High Priest should suffer in the outer court, but that He should pass into heaven to present his righteousness before God for our justification. Both, therefore, as the evidence of the acceptance of his satisfaction on our behalf, and as a necessary step to secure the application of the merits of his sacrifice, the resurrection of Christ was absolutely essential, even for our justification.[1]

The fact is, "if Christ has not been raised, your faith is worthless; you are still in your sins" (1 Cor. 15:17). If Jesus did not rise from the dead, then sin won the victory over Christ and therefore continues to be victorious over us all. If Jesus remained dead, then when we die, we too will remain dead and damned to eternal punishment. If Christ did not defeat death, His death was useless, our faith in Him is useless, and

God still holds our sins against us. If Christ was not raised by God, then He did not reconcile us to God, redeem us from the penalty of our sin, bring about the forgiveness of sins, or provide the one and perfect sacrifice for sins. If all of those things were true, then His death would be nothing more than the heroic death of a noble martyr, the pathetic death of a madman, or the execution of a fraud. All men would be damned and eternal heaven empty of all but God and the holy angels.

But God *did* raise Jesus from the dead (see Rom. 4:25). His death *did* pay the price for our sins, and His resurrection proved it. When God raised Jesus from the dead, He demonstrated that His Son had offered the full satisfaction for sin that the law demands.

Not only that, Christ's resurrection proves His power over the supreme penalty of sin—death. The grave could not hold Jesus because He had conquered death, and His conquest over death bequeaths eternal life to every person who trusts in Him. The apostle Peter said, "God raised Him up again, putting an end to the agony of death, since it was impossible for Him to be held in its power" (Acts 2:24).

Death was powerless to hold Jesus for several reasons. First, death could not contain Him because He possessed divine power. Jesus was "the resurrection and the life" (John 11:25) who died "that through death He might render powerless him who had the power of death, that is, the devil" (Heb. 2:14).

Satan's power to kill us had to be broken for us to be brought to God, so in His resurrection, our Lord robbed Satan of his supreme strategy. Death is a powerful satanic weapon, but God has a weapon that is more powerful—eternal life—and with it Jesus destroyed death. The way to eternal life is through resurrection, so Jesus went into death, through death, and came out the other side.

Divine promise was a second reason that death was not able to hold Jesus. John 2:18–22 records the following dialogue:

> The Jews then said to Him, "What sign do You show us as your authority for doing these things?" Jesus answered them, "Destroy this temple, and in three days I will raise it up." The Jews then said, "It took forty-six years to build this temple, and will You raise it up in three days?" But He was speaking of the temple of His body. So when He was raised from the dead, His disciples remembered that He said this; and they believed the Scripture and the word which Jesus had spoken.

"Thus it is written," our Lord told the disciples, "that the Christ would suffer and rise again from the dead the third day" (Luke 24:46). Jesus Himself, who is the Truth, the incarnate God who cannot lie, promised that He would rise from the dead.

Third, death could not hold Him because of divine purpose. God planned that His people be with Him for all eternity.

But to be with Him, they needed to go through death and out the other side, and Jesus had to blaze the trail (see 1 Cor. 15:16–26). He promised the Father He would raise all God's people up and lose none of them but bring them to heaven (see John 6:37–40).

So, by demonstrating His ability to conquer death—a power belonging only to God Himself, the Giver of life—Christ established beyond all doubt that He is God the Son (see Rom. 1:4). Thus the resurrection is proof that Christ's sacrifice was acceptable to God to atone for sins, and as God, He has the power to conquer death and raise the dead.

Daily Challenge

Consider the awesome power of God on our behalf as you read theologian Benjamin B. Warfield's rousing description:

> *That He died manifests His love and His willingness to save. It is His rising again that manifests His power and His ability to save. We cannot be saved by a dead Christ, who undertook but could not perform, and who still lies under the Syrian sky, another martyr of impotent love. To save, He must pass not merely to but through death. If the penalty was fully paid, it cannot have broken Him,*

it must needs have been broken upon Him. The resurrection of Christ is thus the indispensable evidence of His completed work, of His accomplished redemption. . . .

If it is fundamental to Christianity that Jesus should be Lord of all; that God should have highly exalted Him and given Him the name which is above every name; that in the name of Jesus every knee should bow, and every tongue confess Him as Lord: then it is fundamental to Christianity that death too should be subject to Him and it should not be possible for Him to see corruption. This last enemy too He must needs, as Paul asserts, put under His feet; and it is because He has put this last enemy under His feet that we can say with such energy of conviction that nothing can separate us from the love of God which is in Christ Jesus our Lord—not even death itself: and that nothing can harm us and nothing can take away our peace.[2]

Day 20
Our King
Takes His Throne

Christ Jesus is He who died, yes, rather who was raised, who
is at the right hand of God, who also intercedes for us.

Romans 8:34

The bodily resurrection of Jesus was only the beginning of
our Lord's exaltation. Today we will also explore His ascension into heaven, His glorious coronation, and His gracious
intercession for us. And as we do this, we are wise to heed the
questions of D. Martyn Lloyd-Jones:

What is Jesus Christ to us? Where does He come into our
scheme of things? What do we believe concerning Him? Have

we bowed the knee to Him, have we surrendered to Him, do we make this confession concerning Him? Do we say that Jesus of Nazareth, that man who walked about the face of this earth, is Lord, the anointed of God, the One who was set apart to bear the sins of man, including our own? Do we say that it is there alone, in that death, that we find salvation and all that it means, and by which we are reconciled to God? Do we confess that to us He is God and that we worship Him to the glory of God?[1]

As we today examine the remaining steps of Jesus's exaltation, keep in mind that at this moment, the Lord of heaven and earth, who is your own personal Lord and Savior, waits for your fellowship and eager obedience. Read prayerfully, worshipfully. The experience of seeing who He is—the exalted King and Savior who saved you from certain death—should prompt you to renew your commitment to love Him.

Acts 1:9–11 describes the second aspect of Christ's exaltation. After Christ finished His final instructions to His disciples,

He was lifted up while they were looking on, and a cloud received Him out of their sight. And as they were gazing intently into the sky while He was going, behold, two men in white clothing stood beside them. They also said, "Men of Galilee, why do you stand looking into the sky? This Jesus, who has been taken up from you into heaven, will come in just the same way as you have watched Him go into heaven."

Without fanfare, Jesus, in His glorious resurrection body, left this world for the realm of heaven to take His rightful place on the Father's throne at His right hand.

After God raised Jesus from the dead and He ascended into heaven, God "seated Him at His right hand in the heavenly places, far above all rule and authority and power and dominion, and every name that is named, not only in this age but also in the one to come. And He put all things in subjection under His feet" (Eph. 1:20–22). The writer of Hebrews affirmed the same truth: "When He had made purification of sins, He sat down at the right hand of the Majesty on high" (Heb. 1:3). Jesus's sitting down at His Father's right hand signifies at least four things.

First, He sat down as a sign of honor, "that every tongue will confess that Jesus Christ is Lord, to the glory of God the Father" (Phil. 2:11). To be seated at the right hand of the Father is the highest honor.

Second, He sat down as a sign of authority. Peter declared that Christ "is at the right hand of God, having gone into heaven, after angels and authorities and powers had been subjected to Him" (1 Pet. 3:22). Throughout the Old and New Testaments, the right hand is a symbol of preeminence, power, and authority. At the right hand of God Christ acts with the authority and the power of Almighty God over all created things. That's where Jesus went when He had accomplished

His work on the cross, and that's where He rules from today. Matthew 28:18 records Jesus's affirmation of His authority: "All authority has been given to Me in heaven and on earth." Even all judgment was given to Him (see John 5:27). Christ sat down as the sovereign of the universe.

Third, He sat down to rest. There were no seats in the tabernacle or the temple sanctuaries because the old covenant priests offered sacrifices continually throughout the day—their work was never done. But Jesus, the perfect High Priest, sat down because His work was complete. "But He, having offered one sacrifice for sins for all time, sat down at the right hand of God" (Heb. 10:12).

The fourth and final reason He sat down relates directly with the final stage of Christ's exaltation: He sat down to intercede for His people.

Jesus Christ is our High Priest who sat down to plead before God's throne for us. In Romans 8:34 Paul showed the progress of Christ's exaltation: "Christ Jesus is He who died, yes, rather who was raised, who is at the right hand of God, who also intercedes for us." Our Lord is seated at God's right hand at this moment, making intercession for all of us who belong to Him. (We'll examine this vital ministry of Christ in depth on days 22 and 23.)

When Jesus came into the world, He entered a state of being He had never before experienced, the condition of humiliation.

Commentator William Hendricksen's words remind us that
He was restored to glory and exaltation:

> The exaltation is the reversal of humiliation. He who stood
> condemned in relation to the divine law (because of the sin of
> the world which rested on Him) has exchanged this penalty
> for the righteous relation to the law. He who was poor has
> become rich. He who was rejected has been accepted (Rev. 12:5,
> 10). He who learned obedience has entered upon the actual
> administration of the power and authority committed to Him.
>
> As *king*, having by His death, resurrection, and ascension
> achieved and displayed His triumph over His enemies, He now
> holds in His hands the reins of the universe, and rules all things
> in the interest of His church (Eph. 1:22, 23). As *prophet* He
> through His Spirit leads His own in all the truth. And as *priest*
> (high-priest according to the order of Melchizedek) He, on
> the basis of His accomplished atonement, *not only intercedes
> but actually lives forever to make intercession* for those who
> draw near to God through Him.[2]

Wonderfully, all believers will follow Christ in His exaltation. We will enter into His eternal glory. We will also ascend—
not just believers alive at the time of the rapture, but also all
the dead in Christ. In heaven we will experience coronation,
for we will sit with Christ on His throne (see Rev. 3:21). No
longer will we need our Lord's intercessory ministry, because
our transformation will be complete. The path of glory Jesus

followed beginning with His resurrection is the path we will follow as well. That's God's promise.

 Daily Challenge

At no time in His exaltation did Jesus neglect or ignore you; He has paved the way to heaven for you. He has anchored your salvation within the veil in the heavenly Holy of Holies (see Heb. 6:19–20). Don't ever lose sight of that truth. Look to your first love—your exalted Lord—and revel in your coming glory.

Day 21
Every Knee
and Every Tongue

So that at the name of Jesus every knee will bow, of those who are in heaven and on earth and under the earth, and that every tongue will confess that Jesus Christ is Lord, to the glory of God the Father.

Philippians 2:10–11

Because Jesus is the exalted Lord, He gives us the assurance that our redemption is complete and our hope of heaven is secure. We can also be assured that He continually intercedes on our behalf with the Father. A gospel that stops with the humiliation of Christ is incomplete. He must be seen as the resurrected, ascended, crowned, and interceding Christ.

Only one response is appropriate to Christ's exaltation. As our Lord, Jesus Christ deserves our worship. God exalted Him and gave Him the name "Lord" to affirm His authority and cause everyone to bow to Him.

Philippians 2:10 says that at His name, Lord, we are to bow. The subjunctive mood here ("every knee will bow") says that every knee eventually *will* bow—either by choice or by force. By God's grace some are enabled to acknowledge Christ's lordship by choice. Others will bow to Him by force of divine judgment. The phrases "every knee will bow" (v. 10) and "every tongue will confess" (v. 11) are taken from Isaiah 45:23, which strongly emphasizes the sole authority and sovereignty of God. In context, the Lord said:

> There is no other God besides Me,
> A righteous God and a Savior;
> There is none except Me.
> Turn to Me and be saved, all the ends
>   of the earth;
> For I am God, and there is no other.
> I have sworn by Myself,
> The word has gone forth from My mouth
>   in righteousness
> And will not turn back,

that to Me every knee will bow, every tongue
  will swear allegiance.
They will say of Me, "Only in the LORD are
  righteousness and strength."
. . . To whom would you liken Me
And make Me equal and compare Me,
That we would be alike?
Those who lavish gold from the purse
And weigh silver on the scale
Hire a goldsmith, and he makes it into a god;
They bow down, indeed they worship it.
They lift it upon the shoulder and carry it;
They set it in its place and it stands there.
It does not move from its place.
Though one may cry to it, it cannot answer;
It cannot deliver him from his distress.
Remember this, and be assured;
Recall it to mind, you transgressors.
Remember the former things long past,
For I am God, and there is no other;
I am God, and there is no one like Me,
Declaring the end from the beginning,
And from ancient times things which have
  not been done,
Saying, "My purpose will be established,
And I will accomplish all My good pleasure."
    (Isa. 45:21–24; 46:5–10)

Isaiah 45–46 clearly establishes that God is Lord and sovereign. Paul is saying that what is true of God is true of the Lord Jesus Christ—every knee will bow and every tongue will confess that He is Lord of all. We know Him as the Lord and we know Him as Jesus, the name associated with His saving work (see Matt. 1:21). But He must be known as both to be known at all. One receives the gift of salvation by receiving Jesus, the humiliated Savior, and bowing the knee to Him as majestic, sovereign Lord.

Philippians 2:10 affirms that the entire intelligent universe is called to worship Christ: "Those who are in heaven and on earth and under the earth."

The heavenly group consists of the angels and men. They already acknowledge that Jesus is Lord. The angelic group consists of God's holy, elect angels—the unfallen seraphim, cherubim, and myriads of other angels who worship God in heaven. The spirits of redeemed believers are the triumphant Old Testament and New Testament saints now in the presence of Christ: "the general assembly and church of the firstborn who are enrolled in heaven . . . the spirits of the righteous made perfect" (Heb. 12:23).

The earthly group is made up of both believers and unbelievers who are still alive. As believers we submit to Christ as Lord and Savior, having followed the pattern of Romans 10:9: "If you confess with your mouth Jesus as Lord, and believe in your heart that God raised Him from the dead, you will be saved."

The disobedient on earth will also bow before Jesus Christ, but by compulsion. Second Thessalonians 1:7–9 says, "When the Lord Jesus will be revealed from heaven with His mighty angels in flaming fire, [He will deal] out retribution to those who do not know God and to those who do not obey the gospel of our Lord Jesus. These will pay the penalty of eternal destruction, away from the presence of the Lord and from the glory of His power." When Jesus returns to subdue the earth, He will remove the wicked from the earth, cast them into hell, and establish His kingdom.

"Under the earth" refers to the place of eternal punishment, which is occupied by demons and evil men. They too will acknowledge the lordship of Christ—not by enjoying His reign but by bearing the unending expression of His wrath in eternal torment.

Jesus Christ is Lord everywhere in the universe. Therefore "every tongue will confess that Jesus Christ is Lord" (Phil. 2:11). To "confess" means to acknowledge, affirm, or agree. Everyone—demons, men, holy angels, glorified saints—will acknowledge His lordship. History is moving toward the day when Jesus will be acknowledged by all as the supreme ruler of the universe. He already sits in the seat of power but has not yet brought the fallen universe fully under His authority. We live in days of grace, during which He brings men and women to acknowledge Him as Lord willingly rather than by force. But one day He will subdue everything in the universe: "When all things are subjected to Him, then the Son Himself also will be subjected to the One who subjected all things to Him, that God may be all in all" (1 Cor. 15:28). God is glorified in anything that lifts up or exalts the Son. That's what Paul was referring to when he said that when all acknowledge that Jesus Christ is Lord, it redounds "to the glory of God the Father" (Phil. 2:11).

Daily Challenge

That Jesus is Lord is the most important confession of Christianity. He is to be confessed as Lord by one's mouth and in one's heart. D. Martyn Lloyd-Jones wrote:

> *How easy it is to turn the New Testament into a philosophy or a set of rules and regulations and a scheme for life and living, a general outlook. . . . I do not accept the Christian philosophy primarily; I accept Him. I believe on Him, I bow my knee to Him, the Person. I make a statement about the individual; Jesus Christ is Lord, He is my Lord; it is a personal relationship, and a personal confession.[1]*

Does He continually have the preeminence in your life?

Day 22
Our Sympathetic High Priest

> We do not have a high priest who cannot sympathize with our weaknesses, but One who has been tempted in all things as we are, yet without sin. Therefore let us draw near with confidence to the throne of grace, so that we may receive mercy and find grace to help in time of need.
>
> Hebrews 4:15–16

In the face of this world's trials and temptations, Satan doesn't want us to look to Christ; he wants us to depend on ourselves and our long list of man-made solutions. When we do, he attacks in two areas. First, he'll cause us to doubt God's power and view our trials and temptations as too overwhelming, even for God. Once he has us focusing on our impossible circumstances instead of trusting the wisdom, power, and purpose of the Lord and has successfully diverted us from pursuing our relationship with Christ, he has led us into a more desperate condition.

Satan also assaults us by causing us to doubt God's forgiveness in our ongoing struggle with sin. While Christ's death and resurrection eradicated the penalty of sin, we have not yet escaped its presence. Daily sin attempts to regain its dominion over us through the flesh. Satan wants us to forget that "having been freed from sin, [we] became slaves of righteousness" (Rom. 6:18). By bringing continual accusations, Satan, if so allowed, will deflect a believer's focus off the One who already paid the penalty for those very sins and cause him or her to lose heart, assurance, joy, and peace.

As a Christian, you don't have to succumb to the wiles of the devil (see 1 Pet. 5:8–10). We have a living Lord who is all-powerful, and there is no trial too hard for us in His strength (see 2 Cor. 10:13; Phil. 4:19). And we have a risen Savior who conquered sin and Satan for us and has all the resources necessary to resist the devil and his assaults on us. A couple of days ago we noted that the final phase of Christ's exaltation is His current ministry of intercession for Christians. It is in this very ministry, as He fulfills the role of our sympathetic High Priest, that our Lord in heaven comes to our aid in everything, so that we are more than conquerors (see Rom. 8:37). Jude 24 says, "Now to Him who is able to keep you from stumbling, and to make you stand in the presence of His glory blameless with great joy." And it is that very ministry that ought to motivate you, if you have forgotten all He does for you each and every day, to return to your first love.

For a priest in the Old Testament to truly represent the people, he had to be "taken from among men" (Heb. 5:1). Only another man could be subject to the temptations of men, experience suffering like men, and thereby be able to represent them to God in an understanding and compassionate way. Jesus Christ could not be a true high priest unless He were a man. In sending His Son, Jesus Christ, God entered into the human world and felt everything that men will ever feel that "He might become a merciful and faithful high priest" (2:17). Thus Jesus is our perfect priest, "For we do not have a high priest who cannot sympathize with our weaknesses, but One who has been tempted in all things as we are, yet without sin" (4:15).

Jesus has an unequaled capacity for sympathizing with us in every danger, trial, or situation that comes our way, because He's been through it all: "Since He Himself was tempted in that which He has suffered, He is able to come to the aid of those who are tempted" (2:18). Jesus had perfect awareness of the evil and dangers of sin. Contrary to what we are inclined to think, His divinity made His temptations and trials immeasurably harder for Him to endure than ours are for us, because He never yielded, thus feeling their full assault.

There is a degree of temptation we will never experience because we will succumb long before we reach that point. Since Jesus never sinned, He took the full extent of all that Satan could throw at Him. Since He never succumbed, He experienced every temptation to the maximum. And no human has ever been perfectly holy as He was, so no human has ever had the sensitivity to sin He had. He knows everything we know, and a great deal we do not know, about temptation, testing, and pain. The Greek word translated "weaknesses" (4:15) refers to all the natural limitations of humanity, including liability to sin. Jesus knew firsthand the drive of human nature toward sin. His humanity was His battleground. He was victorious but not without the most intense temptation, grief, and anguish.

Despite the intensity of His battle, Jesus was "without sin." The two Greek words translated "without sin" express the complete absence of sin. Though He was relentlessly tempted to sin, not the slightest bit of sin ever entered His mind, let alone was ever expressed in His words and actions.

Jesus's righteous response to the temptation of sin qualifies Him to sympathize with us. Because He knows us and our struggles intimately, Jesus leads us down the path of victory over them. "No temptation has overtaken you but such as is common to man; and God is faithful, who will not allow you to be tempted beyond what you are able, but with the temptation will provide the way of escape also, so that you will be able to endure it" (1 Cor. 10:13).

Salvation Army evangelist Frederick Booth-Tucker certainly knew the helping hand of Christ. He once preached a message in Chicago on the sympathy of Jesus. Afterward a man came forward and asked him how he could talk about a loving, understanding, sympathetic God. "If your wife had just died, like mine has," the man said, "and your babies were crying for their mother who would never come back, you wouldn't be saying what you're saying."

A few days later, Booth-Tucker's wife was killed in a train accident. After the Chicago funeral service the bereaved preacher looked down into the silent face of his wife and then turned to those who were attending. "The other day when I was here," he said, "a man told me that, if my wife had just died and my children were crying for their mother, I would not be able to say that Christ was understanding and sympathetic, or that He was sufficient for every need. If that man is here, I want to tell him that Christ is sufficient. My heart is broken, it is crushed, but it has a song, and Christ put it there. I want to tell that man that Jesus Christ speaks comfort to me today."[1] The man was there, and he came and knelt beside the casket while Booth-Tucker introduced him to Jesus Christ.

Knowledge and sympathy for another's struggles are important, but if you don't have the resources to help someone in that struggle, your sympathy is limited. While I can pray for someone who is going through some spiritual struggle and empathize with his or her pain, I don't have the power or the resources to change the situation that caused the trouble. But Jesus, our High Priest, does have the resources. "Therefore let us draw near with confidence to the throne of grace, so that we may receive mercy and may find grace to help in time of need" (Heb. 4:16).

The "throne of grace" is another name for God's throne. It would have been a throne of judgment if Jesus had not sprinkled His blood upon it and transformed it into a throne of grace for all who trust in Him.

There is a distinction between "receiving mercy" and "finding grace." Mercy is compassion toward our misery, and grace becomes the source of transforming power to overcome that misery. We can approach God's throne with eagerness and confidence, because Christ is there interceding on our behalf, having made atonement for our sins. It is a throne of grace because He will dispense the grace we need for every concern of life.

Daily Challenge

According to 1 John 4:19, "We love, because He first loved us." Your only hope of reinvigorating your love for Christ is to understand the depth of His love for you.

Day 23
Our Advocate with the Father

If anyone sins, we have an Advocate with the Father, Jesus Christ the righteous; and He Himself is the propitiation for our sins; and not for ours only, but also for those of the whole world.

1 John 2:1–2

Satan often calls into question the reality of our salvation because of our sin. But because of the reality described in the passage above, we can turn to Christ. "If we confess our sins, He is faithful and righteous to forgive us our sins and to cleanse us from all unrighteousness" (1 John 1:9). One aspect of Christ's function as our High Priest in heaven is His advocacy before the Father.

When we sin, Jesus is our "Advocate." That word is a translation of the Greek word *paracletos*, the same word that is translated "Helper" or "Comforter" in reference to the Holy Spirit (see John 15:26). *Paracletos* means "a lawyer for the defense" or "someone called alongside to help."

Satan is unrelenting in his efforts to accuse believers before God. Revelation 12:10 says he is before the throne of God day and night accusing God's children. If we were to depict this scene in a courtroom setting, Satan would be the prosecutor and Christ the lawyer for our defense. But Satan has no case against us—it can never get a hearing in God's court—because our Advocate has Himself paid the penalty for our sin. The Almighty Judge has already declared us not guilty. The apostle Paul asked, "Who will bring a charge against God's elect?" (Rom. 8:33) after God Himself has already justified them. Satan can't successfully accuse us, because Christ has removed all our sins from the record. There is no condemnation ever to those in Christ (see Rom. 8:1).

"Jesus Christ the righteous . . . is the propitiation [appeasement] for our sins" (1 John 2:1–2). When we are accused, Jesus doesn't plead our innocence to God; rather, He pleads His own righteousness, which has been granted to us by grace through faith. God's hatred of sin had to be appeased, and Jesus Christ's death paid for our sins. Thus He satisfied God's justice.

Because Christ paid the penalty for sin and reconciled us to God as a result, Paul said that "we have obtained our introduction by faith into this grace in which we stand" (Rom. 5:2). He has given us *permanent* access to God. That's the idea behind the word "stand" (*histemi*). Although faith is necessary for salvation, it is God's grace working in the believer that generates that faith. We are not saved by divine grace and then preserved through human effort. To the Philippian believers Paul declared, "He who began a good work in you will perfect it until the day of Christ Jesus" (Phil. 1:6).

We've already established that believers will fall into sin, but their sin is not more powerful than God's grace. They are the very sins for which Jesus paid the full penalty. If no sin a person commits before salvation is too great for Christ's atoning death to cover, surely no sin he or she commits after salvation is too great to be covered. Paul declared, "For if while we were enemies we were reconciled to God through the death of His Son, much more, having been reconciled, we shall be saved by His life" (Rom. 5:10).

Paul means that if a dying Savior could bring us to salvation, surely a living Savior can keep us in His grace. If God had the power and the grace to redeem us in the first place, how much more does He have the power and the grace to keep us redeemed? Our Savior not only delivers us from sin and its judgment but also delivers us from uncertainty and doubt about that deliverance.

How can a Christian, whose past and future salvation are secured by God, be insecure? If sin was no barrier to the beginning of our redemption, how can it become a barrier to its completion?

That being the case:

> If God is for us, who is against us? He who did not spare His own Son, but delivered Him over for us all, how will He not also with Him freely give us all things? Who will bring a charge against God's elect? God is the one who justifies; who is the one who condemns? Christ Jesus is He who died, yes, rather who was raised, who is at the right hand of God, who also intercedes for us. (Rom. 8:31–34)

Although His work of atonement is finished, Christ's continuing ministry of intercession for those saved through His sacrifice will continue without interruption until every redeemed soul is safe in heaven. Just as Isaiah prophesied, "He poured out Himself to death, and was numbered with the transgressors; yet He Himself bore the sin of many, and interceded for the transgressors" (Isa. 53:12). He "is able also to save forever those who draw near to God through Him, since He always lives to make intercession for them" (Heb. 7:25). Jesus pledged that He would lose none of God's elect but bring them all to glory (see John 6:37–40).

The securing of our salvation is the function of Jesus's perpetual intercession for us. We can no more keep ourselves saved than we can save ourselves in the first place. But just as Jesus had the power to save us, He has the power to keep us. Constantly, eternally, perpetually Jesus Christ intercedes for us before His Father. Through Christ we are able to "stand in the presence of His glory blameless with great joy" (Jude 24). In His Son we are now blameless in the Father's sight. When we are glorified, we will be blameless in His presence. Don't let Satan get away with His accusations—you are secure in Christ. Through our remaining days on earth and throughout all eternity, our gracious Lord will hold us safe in His everlasting love by His everlasting power.

Pastor Peter Lewis has provided a fitting summary of Christ's interceding on behalf of His own:

> Jesus Christ in his mediation does not operate as a third party, *moving between* God and believers, as though God would always be unapproachable; rather, he operates as *one* with God and his people, in whom believers are brought face to face with a Father who loves them, who delights to receive them, and who rejoices to make their persons and their prayers, their worship and their lives accepted in the beloved Son.
>
> I once heard of a picture which perfectly illustrates this. It was a large, typically Victorian religious piece of work, but the artist showed a striking degree of spiritual insight as well as originality in his composition. The scene was a storm on the lake of first-century Galilee. The foreground was dominated by a representation of Jesus's terrified disciples, rowing furiously

through huge waves which threatened to engulf and overturn them at any moment. There seemed at first to be nothing else—no relief in the scene of fear and extreme danger. Then one's eye was taken by a shaft of sunlight through the storm-clouds to a rocky hillside on the shore. And there one saw, kneeling among the rocks, a praying figure. Many artists had painted the later scene, Christ walking on the water "in the fourth watch of the night" (Matt. 14:22–23), but this artist had captured a reality just as profound when he depicted an earlier stage in the drama: Christ praying in the hills (v. 23) while His followers were battling the storm (v. 24)![1]

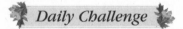 *Daily Challenge*

With that picture in mind, why do so many believers, when faced with trials and temptation, go anywhere but to God's throne? Christ is there, ever ready to strengthen you, comfort you, and restore you. He is prepared to receive the sin-stained heart that you bring to Him and to clean it. And He is ever ready to dry your tears. All the resources are in Him. But you need to pursue Him to take advantage of those resources. To begin to do that, you need to return to your first love.

Day 24

Following Our Lord in Suffering

> For you have been called for this purpose, since Christ also
> suffered for you, leaving you an example for you to follow in
> His steps.
>
> 1 Peter 2:21

If there is ever a "time of need" in our lives when it is appropriate to "draw near with confidence to the throne of grace,
so that we may receive mercy and find grace to help" (Heb.
4:16), it's in the midst of our most difficult trials. Suffering is
a special type of circumstance in which we must draw upon
the lordship and example of Jesus Christ. In fact, it is often

as we follow Him through suffering that we experience our deepest intimacy with our Lord.

In his devotional studies on the life of Christ, titled *The Second Person*, commentator Lehman Strauss wrote:

> Not one person in all the world is exempt from sorrow. Philosophers of every age have acknowledged it. Biographers, no matter how shallow the treatise, have recorded it. Experience has confirmed it. From the fact of suffering there is no escape. It sinks its fangs deeply into rich and poor, high and low, saved and lost.
>
> Except for natural causes and war, perhaps the greatest injuries have been inflicted upon men because of their religious convictions. Since the vicious slaying of John the Baptist . . . there has been no intermission in the attacks on the followers of Christ. History is revealing in its gruesome accounts of human suffering inflicted upon thousands of His disciples.[1]

While that is what we most often associate with those who suffer for Christ, Strauss identified a subtler but nonetheless real type of suffering:

> There is the torture of the mind and the agony of the soul— that escapeless, gnawing suffering which no person can truly share. Records of this are uncommon; words do not adequately portray it. Are you brokenhearted because one with whom you shared your confidences has betrayed you?

Are you misunderstood and do your associates not value your taste nor your choices? . . . Have friends or loved ones forsaken you? . . . Do others torment you until you sting with shame? . . . Do the injustices done you inflame you until you think you must retaliate? . . . Do you believe no one cares? . . . Do you feel that the burden you must carry is too great?[2]

In our safe, secure society, it is unlikely we will ever suffer to the same degree as the martyrs and saints did who came before us, yet to that last series of questions Strauss posed, we all can relate. Every Christian has experienced at least one if not all those types of sorrows throughout his or her lifetime. How we respond is the true test of our faith and will reveal the depth of our relationship to Christ.

The Christian life is a call to glory through a journey of suffering. That's because those in Christ are inevitably at odds with their culture and society, since all Satan-energized systems actively oppose Christ and His followers. The apostle John said a person can't love both God and the world (see 1 John 2:15), and James said that "whoever wishes to be a friend of the world makes himself an enemy of God" (James 4:4).

Those who love Christ are an open rebuke to the society in which they live. That was the apostle Peter's point when he described Christians as "a chosen race, a royal priesthood, a holy nation, a people for God's own possession . . . [who] proclaim the excellencies of Him who has called [them] out of darkness into His marvelous light" (1 Pet. 2:9). Our dark world will resent and be hostile toward anyone who represents the Lord Jesus Christ in that way. That resentment and hostility may be felt at certain times and places more than others, but it is always present to some extent.

Fortunately, we have One to whom we can turn when we suffer—the very One who suffered for us: the Lord Jesus Christ. Peter wrote, "For you have been called for this purpose, since Christ also suffered for you, leaving you an example for you to follow in His steps" (v. 21). Peter's model of how to respond to suffering was Jesus Christ, and we need to follow His example. Our Lord's was the most unjust execution ever perpetrated on a human being. Yet from it we learn that even though a person may be perfectly within the will of God—greatly loved and gifted, flawlessly righteous and obedient—he may still experience unjust suffering. Like Jesus, he may be misunderstood, misrepresented, hated, persecuted, and even murdered. In His death Christ set the standard of how to respond to unjust persecution.

We follow His pattern by walking "in His steps." We are to walk in Christ's footprints because He traveled a righteous path, and along that path He endured unjust suffering. Some suffer more than others, but all who follow Christ will experience suffering to some degree.

The writer of Hebrews emphasized this particular role of Christ when he said, "It was fitting for [God] . . . in bringing many sons to glory, to perfect the author of their salvation through sufferings" (Heb. 2:10). The Greek word for "author" is *archegos*, which literally means "pioneer" or "leader." This word was commonly used in classical Greek to describe a pioneer who blazed a trail for others to follow. The *archegos* never stood at the rear giving orders but rather was always out front leading and setting the example. Christ is our supreme pioneer, our perfect leader and example, who leads us down the path of suffering and to victory on the other side.

First Peter 2:21 begins with the phrase "For you have been called for this purpose." The connective "for" points back to the last part of verse 20: "If when you do what is right and suffer for it you patiently endure it, this finds favor with God." Christians are to endure suffering because it pleases God.

First Peter 5:10 explains further: "After you have suffered for a little while, the God of all grace, who called you to His eternal glory in Christ, will Himself perfect, confirm, strengthen and establish you." Suffering is God's way of maturing His people spiritually. He is pleased when we patiently endure the suffering that comes our way.

Peter also said, "You greatly rejoice, even though now for a little while, if necessary, you have been distressed by various trials, so that the proof of your faith, being more precious than gold which is perishable, even though tested by fire, may be found to result in praise and glory and honor at the revelation of Jesus

Christ" (1:6–7). God allows suffering as a validation of our faith and to increase our capacity to praise, glorify, and honor God.

Many believers take the wrong approach and look for explanations for their trials elsewhere. Yet it is through those very trials that we deepen our bond with Christ. In Him only can we find the inner peace and joy to see our trials through to the end (see James 1:2–3). Rejoicing in our first love helps us view our trials from our Lord's perspective. That was what Paul was aiming at when he said that our "momentary, light affliction is producing for us an eternal weight of glory far beyond all comparison" (2 Cor. 4:17; see also v. 18). In other words, as you endure a trial, focus on its eternal impact, not its temporary consequence.

Daily Challenge

Christ Himself understood that this was God's plan. To the disciples on the road to Emmaus, He said, "O foolish men and slow of heart to believe in all that the prophets have spoken! Was it not necessary for the Christ to suffer these things and to enter into His glory?" (Luke 24:25–26). If our Lord had to suffer to enter into His future glory, so also we, journeying along the path to glory, ought to expect to suffer.

Day 25

Our Lord's Response to Suffering

[Christ] committed no sin, nor was any deceit found in His mouth; and while being reviled, He did not revile in return; while suffering, He uttered no threats, but kept entrusting Himself to Him who judges righteously.

1 Peter 2:22–23

Our Lord's suffering on the cross was certainly prominent in Peter's mind because he personally witnessed his Lord's pain, though from afar. The passage above takes us to the cross, explaining in the process the meaning of Isaiah 53—the clearest Old Testament chapter on the suffering of the Messiah. As we learn from our Lord's example how to respond to suffering, let us also remember that His present ministry is to provide us "grace to help in time of need" (Heb. 4:16). Not only does Jesus lead us through suffering as our example but He also accompanies and supports us as our sympathetic High Priest.

Peter first said that Christ "committed no sin, nor was any deceit found in His mouth" (1 Pet. 2:22). Isaiah 53:9 says that "He [the Messiah] had done no violence." *Violence* is translated "lawlessness" in the Septuagint, the Greek version of the Hebrew Old Testament. The translators understood that the violence spoken of in Isaiah 53:9 is violence, or sin, against God's law, which "is lawlessness" (1 John 3:4). Peter, under the inspiration of the Holy Spirit, understood the violence spoken of in Isaiah 53:9 in the same way. Peter's point was that in spite of the unjust treatment Christ had to endure, He committed no sin. He was impeccable—He did not and could not sin (see 1 Pet. 1:19).

Isaiah 53:9 adds, "Nor was there any deceit in His mouth." The Hebrew word translated "deceit" can refer to any sin of the tongue, such as deception, innuendo, or slander. What we say, more than any other aspect of human behavior, reveals what's in our hearts (see Mark 7:21). That's what led James to say, "If anyone does not stumble in what he says, he is a perfect man" (James 3:2). Jesus never offended in what He said, indicating His perfection.

In all the circumstances of His ministry on earth, our Lord was absolutely sinless. He was "tempted in all things as we are, yet [was] without sin" (Heb. 4:15; see also 2 Cor. 5:21; Heb. 7:26). Consequently He was the most unjustly treated person who ever lived. He is the perfect model of how we are to respond to unjust treatment.

Peter next reflected on what Isaiah 53:7 says of the Messiah: "He was oppressed and He was afflicted, yet He did not open His mouth; like a lamb that is led to slaughter, and like a sheep that is silent before its shearers, so He did not open His mouth." That reflects the attitude of Jesus before His tormentors: "While being reviled, He did not revile in return" (1 Pet. 2:23).

The Greek word translated "reviled" pictures the continual piling up of one abuse on top of another. Jesus was consistent in His response to such treatment: He was silent (see Matt. 26:57–68; 27:11–14; Mark 14:53–65; 15:1–5; Luke 23:8–9). Christians, like their Master, are never to abuse those who abuse them.

Jesus "uttered no threats" in the face of incredible suffering (1 Pet. 2:23). He was the Incarnate God—the Creator and Sustainer of the universe—and as such had the power to send His tormentors into eternal flames. Yet instead of threatening them, He said, "Father, forgive them; for they do not know what they are doing" (Luke 23:34). Christ died for sinners, including those who persecuted Him. He knew that the glory of salvation could be achieved only through the path of suffering, so He accepted His suffering without bitterness, anger, or a spirit of retaliation.

First Peter 3:9 says that Christians are not to be "returning evil for evil or insult for insult, but giving a blessing instead." That was Jesus's attitude: He "kept entrusting Himself to Him who judges righteously" (2:23). The word translated "entrusting" (*paradidomi*) means "to hand over for someone to keep." In every instance of suffering, our Lord handed over the circumstance and Himself to God.

Christ's last words on the cross reveal His trust in God: "Father, into Your hands I commit My spirit" (Luke 23:46). He was confident in God's righteous judgment and the glory that would be His. That allowed Him to calmly accept tremendous suffering. We are to respond in the same way when confronted with unjust persecution on the job or in our families or other relationships. A retaliatory spirit exposes our lack of confidence in God's ability to make things right in His own time. That kind of response also calls into question the reality of our commitment to Christ. Unbelievers will be turned off by those who claim to love Christ yet act like any other unregenerate person. When we entrust ourselves to God as the righteous judge, we are following Christ's example by looking to God for vindication, exaltation, and reward.

If you're a Christian, expect to suffer. As believers, we are aliens and strangers in the world, waging war against fleshly lusts and being slandered and persecuted. We must expect to suffer in the name of the One who endured all manner of suffering for us. The central thrust of Peter's message is to remind us of the necessity of suffering. When in the midst of suffering we sin in thought, word, or deed by retaliating, we lose our victory and damage our testimony.

I believe that in days to come Christians will become increasingly unpopular with secular society. Strong stands for the truth of Scripture and the gospel message may soon become intolerable. That will result in unjust treatment, which ought to drive us to passages like 1 Peter 2:21–23 for reassurance. Here we learn that, like our Lord, we are to walk the path of suffering to attain the glory of reward and exaltation in the future. That realization surely prompted the martyr Stephen to fix his eyes on Jesus in glory and ask God to forgive his murderers (see Acts 7:54–60). Stephen entrusted himself to God, knowing that the Lord would vindicate him.

In May 1555, Bishop Hugh Latimer, soon to be burned at the stake for his antipapal, Reformed convictions, wrote, "Die once we must; how and where, we know not. . . . Here is not our home; let us therefore accordingly consider things, having always before our eyes that heavenly Jerusalem, and the way thereto in persecution."[1] Later that year both Latimer and his friend Ridley were fed to the flames, but not until Latimer—astonishingly composed—said to his colleague, "Be of good comfort, Master Ridley, and play the man. We shall this day light such a candle, by God's grace, in England, as I trust shall never be put out."[2]

If we are ever to deepen our relationship to Christ, we must be willing to share in His sufferings. That was certainly Paul's perspective when he expressed the hope "that I may know Him and the power of His resurrection and the fellowship of His sufferings, being conformed to His death" (Phil. 3:10).

 Daily Challenge

You may never have the opportunity to glorify God in the manner Latimer did, yet as you remember how Christ suffered for you, I hope you'll regard each momentary light affliction God brings your way as an opportunity to glorify Christ and rely on His lordship. When the suffering comes, God will be gracious. And when you endure it with patience, you will reap maturity in Christ for the present and a greater capacity to glorify God in the life to come. Charles Haddon Spurgeon understood this when he said:

> *When the pangs shoot through our body, and ghastly death appears in view, people see the patience of the*

dying Christian. Our infirmities become the black velvet on which the diamond of God's love glitters all the more brightly. *Thank God I can suffer! Thank God I can be made the object of shame and contempt, for in this way God shall be glorified.*[3]

Day 26
Love and Obedience

If you love Me, you will keep My commandments.

John 14:15

A famous lyric from an old, popular song says, "Love and marriage go together like a horse and carriage." When it comes to the spiritual realm, love and obedience also go together—one pulls the other. In this relationship, however, love is the driving force behind obedience, because the biblical concept of love has nothing to do with emotion or sentimentality; it has everything to do with an act of the will. Jesus said it best: "If you love Me, you will keep My commandments. . . . He who has My commandments and keeps them, is the one who loves

Me" (John 14:15, 21). Obedience to Christ and His Word is the ultimate proof of the reality of our love to Christ.

The Old Testament saints understood that kind of commitment. Deuteronomy 6:5 says, "You shall love the LORD your God with all your heart and with all your soul and with all your might." Their devotion to God was an all-consuming and wholehearted priority. Loving and obeying God were not optional. Neither were worshiping and serving Him.

Jesus affirmed that priority when a conniving lawyer asked Him which commandment in the Law was the greatest. Jesus said, "'You shall love the Lord your God with all your heart, and with all your soul, and with all your mind.' This is the great and foremost commandment" (Matt. 22:37–38). That command is no less important for us. A consuming love for the Lord Jesus Christ ought to be the priority of our lives. Peter summed up our priority when, speaking of Christ, he said, "Though you have not seen Him, you love Him" (1 Pet. 1:8). Paul said that we ought to "love our Lord Jesus Christ with incorruptible love" (Eph. 6:24). Love for Christ even takes precedence over our closest human relationships. "He who loves father or mother more than Me is not worthy of Me; and he who loves son or daughter more than Me is not worthy of Me" (Matt. 10:37). Ultimately, lack of love to Christ calls into question the genuineness of one's salvation. "If anyone does not love the Lord, he is to be accursed" (1 Cor. 16:22).

Puritan Thomas Vincent described the ways in which our obedience reveals the reality of our love to Christ:

> Your love to Christ is known by your obedience unto Christ. If Christ is your beloved, He is also your Lord; if you have true affection for Him, you will yield subjection unto Him. If you love Christ, you are careful to please Christ; you are not the servants of the flesh, to take care to please the flesh, but you are the servants of Christ to take care, above all persons and all things, to please Christ. If you love Christ, you are fearful of giving just occasion of offense unto men but, above all, you are fearful of displeasing and offending your Lord. Do you labor so to walk that you may please Christ in the way of sincere and universal obedience? Are you hearty in your obedience unto Christ? Have you a respect to all His commandments? Is it your grief that you fall short in your obedience unto Christ? If you can say in the presence of the Lord and your hearts (do not give your tongues the lie) that you do not live and allow yourselves in the practice of any known sin which Christ forbids, nor in the neglect of any known duty which Christ commands, this is sure evidence of true love to Jesus Christ.[1]

When I look at Christ's church, I rarely see that kind of devotion, that kind of commitment, that sheer abandonment to divine priorities. In many ways we give equal, if not greater, affection and devotion to the passing things of this world.

We live in a day when the vast majority of people in our world lack convictions about what their priorities ought to be because they are constantly bombarded by a myriad of options. Each day we make choices about what to eat, what to wear, and how to entertain ourselves. In the process we've allowed our faith and love for Christ to be reduced to a single choice among the many on our list of options. To many, what was once the priority on Sunday morning—going to church—is now just one of several choices. After all, since Sunday is a day off from work or school for most people, why not just play golf, take a drive, go to brunch, take in a ball game or a movie, go on a picnic, or just simply spend the day around the house and tinker or watch television?

In the midst of all the alternatives, Christians have allowed to slip the reality that their faith is ultimately made up of specific nonoptionals. Instead of loving Him with all their being, many believers have learned to love the Lord Jesus Christ selectively. They may verbalize their love for Him, but the real question is whether or not it makes a difference in the way they live. They are willing to love the Lord if the price isn't too high, if it makes them feel comfortable, or if that's the best option at the time. Thomas Vincent described what that lack of love to Christ communicates:

> It is observed, and it is greatly to be lamented, that there is, of late years, a great decay in the power of godliness among those

that are sincere; and is it not evident in the great decay of love, even in true Christians, unto Jesus Christ? . . . Is it not evident that you have but little love to Christ when He is but little in your thoughts and meditations? . . . You can think often of your food, but how little do your thoughts feed upon Christ, who is the Bread of Life? You can often think of your raiment, but how little do you think of the robes of Christ's righteousness? You can think often of your earthly friends, but how little do you think of Jesus Christ, your friend in heaven? . . .

Moreover, does it not argue little love to Christ that you speak so little *of* Him and *for* Him in your conversing one with another? If you had much love to Christ, would not this love breathe forth more in your discourses? . . . Out of the abundance of the heart, the mouth will speak of their riches. Such as have much love to pleasures will be often speaking of that subject; such as love their friends much will be often speaking and commending them when they are in company. And when you speak but little of Christ, it is a sign that you love Him but little.[2]

Amazingly, Vincent wrote that in the seventeenth century, over three hundred years ago, when people did not have the number of alternatives we have today. The problem for most Christians is not that they have altogether stopped loving Christ, for that would betray an unredeemed life, but that they have been diverted from their first love by the world's priorities.

Daily Challenge

We need to return to our first love. To do that (as I men-tioned at the beginning of this book), we need to follow the three steps outlined by the Lord in Revelation 2:5: remember, repent, and repeat. In the previous daily read-ings, I've endeavored to help you remember by recalling for you who Christ is, what He has done, and what He is now doing for you. In the remainder of this book we'll deal with our Lord's last two commands—repent and repeat. For today, though, I encourage you to take inventory of your heart's loves. Where is Jesus Christ on your priority list? What other loves are competing with your first love?

Day 27
When We Fail

If we confess our sins, He is faithful and righteous to forgive us our sins and to cleanse us from all unrighteousness.

1 John 1:9

Over the next two days we'll focus on the necessity of repenting from our failure to love and obey Christ by seeing how our Lord dealt with one who failed Him miserably yet was restored because of his repentant heart: the apostle Peter.

In all the history of redemption, few saints have fallen to the depths of sin and unfaithfulness that Peter did when he denied Jesus the night our Lord was arrested and put on trial for His life. Yet few saints have been so powerfully used by God as Peter was after he repented and was restored. The

Gospel accounts of these two events in Peter's life give us great hope and encouragement that in spite of the severity of our sin against our Lord, He is always waiting to forgive and to restore. Nothing is more devastating to a believer than to realize he or she has denied the Lord by what was said or not said, done or not done. Yet nothing is more exhilarating than knowing God's gracious forgiveness of unfaithfulness after it is confessed and the joy of greater usefulness.

Peter's denial did not happen spontaneously in response to unexpected danger or embarrassment; he laid the groundwork that fateful night through a series of steps that eventually led to his collapse.

Peter's first step was his boast that, "Even though all may fall away because of You, I will never fall away" (Matt. 26:33). That revealed his unfounded self-confidence and directly contradicted His Lord's prediction that *all* the disciples would fall away that very night (see v. 31).

His second step toward his collapse was his blatant denial of Christ's specific prediction: "'Truly I say to you that this very night, before a rooster crows, you will deny Me three times.' Peter said to Him, 'Even if I have to die with You, I will not deny You'" (vv. 34–35).

Peter's next fateful step was his prayerlessness. Jesus took Peter, James, and John with Him to keep watch for Him while He spoke intimately with the Father. But instead of being alert to the coming hour of darkness, they simply went to sleep. When Jesus returned and found them so, He said, "So, you men could not keep watch with Me for one hour? Keep watching and praying that you may not enter into temptation" (vv. 40–41). But they did not take seriously His warnings and were indifferent to His call for prayer.

The next step in Peter's descent was his impulsiveness. When the crowd came to arrest Jesus, Peter tried to decapitate Malchus, the servant of the high priest, but missed and cut off his ear (see v. 51). Peter refused to believe that God's plan was for Christ to suffer and die.

The final step leading to Peter's denial of Christ was his compromise in allowing himself to flee away from His Lord and then linger in a place of danger—the courtyard of the high priest—where his loyalty would be tested beyond his courage. He had boasted too much, spoken too soon, prayed too little, acted too fast, and wandered too far.

Once he arrived in the courtyard, Peter "sat down with the officers to see the outcome" (v. 58) of the trial. Sometime after one o'clock in the morning, about the time the trial began, "a servant-girl came to him and said, 'You too were with Jesus the Galilean'" (v. 69). Peter objected, "Woman, I do not know Him" (Luke 22:57; see also Matt. 26:70).

To escape embarrassment, Peter inconspicuously "went out onto the porch" (Mark 14:68). But in spite of his precautions, "another servant-girl saw him and said to those who were there, 'This man was with Jesus of Nazareth'" (Matt. 26:71). An unidentified man also joined in the accusation, saying, "You are one of them too!" (Luke 22:58). To the girl, Peter "again denied it with an oath, 'I do not know the man'" (Matt. 26:72), and to the man he said, "Man, I am not!" (Luke 22:58). This time he added an oath to his lie. About an hour later (see v. 59), "the bystanders came up and said to Peter, 'Surely you too are one of them; for even the way you talk gives you away'" (Matt. 26:73). Peter could not hide his Galilean accent. Still refusing either to claim or to rely on Jesus, "he began to curse and swear, 'I do not know the man!'" (v. 74). The Greek word translated "to curse" is a strong term that involved pronouncing death on oneself at the hand of God if one were lying.

Then the worst imaginable moment happened. "Immediately, while he was still speaking, a rooster crowed. The Lord turned and looked at Peter" (Luke 22:60–61). The eyes of the Lord must have penetrated Peter's soul, burning deep into his heart the evil of his sin. As if that visual indictment weren't enough, while he stood transfixed by his Lord's eyes, his conscience assaulted him as "Peter remembered the word of the Lord, how He had told him, 'Before a rooster crows today, you will deny Me three times'" (v. 61). Peter's anguish was made even more unbearable.

Fortunately Peter's true character is revealed not in his denial but in his repentance, which began with deep remorse. Overwhelmed by His Savior's love and grace and by his own sin and unfaithfulness, Peter "went out and wept bitterly" (v. 62). It was not until Peter saw the Lord's face and remembered His words that he came to his senses, acknowledged his sin, and repented of his failure. He surrendered his sin to Christ for forgiveness and cleansing.

In spite of his repentance, Peter still had much to learn about what Jesus required of him. He had sinned by what he did in those denials, and he would sin again by what he did not do. After our Lord was resurrected, He told the women who saw Him first to tell His disciples "to leave for Galilee, and there they will see Me" (Matt. 28:10). The Lord appeared to His disciples on two separate occasions before they "proceeded to Galilee, to the mountain which Jesus had designated" (v. 16). John 21:2 tells us that Peter and six other disciples were obedient to a point—they initially went to Galilee and to the mountain the Lord designated. But as time passed and Jesus didn't appear, Peter's impulsiveness took over.

"Simon Peter said to them, 'I am going fishing.' They said to him, 'We will also come with you'" (v. 3). Peter was the leader, and he led the rest of the disciples into outright disobedience of the Lord. He was given a simple command and he disobeyed it; he failed to do what he was told. It's possible Peter thought he was of little use to the Lord so he decided to return to the line of work he knew best. Peter and the other disciples found out quickly the consequences of that disobedience: "They went out and got into the boat; and that night they caught nothing" (v. 3). Peter's self-reliance was useless when it came up against the Lord's will for him. Since he couldn't make it as a disciple, he decided he could still rely on his own ability to catch fish.

But he would quickly discover that this aspect of his life was over.

Daily Challenge

Before continuing with Peter's story, stop and consider the last time you turned to the Lord in repentance from some sin, recommitting yourself to obedience. Did your new commitment continue flawlessly, or did you sometimes falter as Peter did? In these times of transition always remember Your Lord's completed work of redemption on your behalf. And remember His present ministry of mercy and grace in your time of need. If we engage in the regular habit of genuinely confessing our sins—no matter how often we've returned to them—He remains perpetually "faithful and righteous to forgive us our sins and to cleanse us from all unrighteousness" (1 John 1:9).

Day 28
Returning to Love

The love of Christ controls us, having concluded this, that one died for all, therefore all died; and He died for all, so that they who live might no longer live for themselves, but for Him who died and rose again on their behalf.

2 Corinthians 5:14–15

The Lord's timing is always perfect. Peter had grown impatient, but Jesus knew exactly when and how to begin the process of restoring Peter.

When the day was now breaking, Jesus stood on the beach; yet the disciples did not know that it was Jesus. So Jesus said to them, "Children, you do not have any fish, do you?" They answered Him, "No." And He said to them, "Cast the net on the right-hand side of the boat and you will find a catch." So they cast, and then they were not able to haul it in because of the great number of fish. Therefore that disciple [John] whom Jesus loved said to Peter, "It is the Lord." (John 21:4–7)

John may have been recalling the earlier time when Jesus called these same men to follow Him. On that occasion the Lord performed a similar rerouting of the fish in the Sea of Galilee (see Luke 5:4–11). Now, more than three years later, the Lord had to repeat the same lesson. He didn't call them to follow Him so that after He was gone they could return to their old life; He called them so that they might carry on His work of making disciples of all nations (see Matt. 28:19). But to do that, He had to reestablish their priorities.

When Simon Peter heard that it was the Lord, he put his outer garment on (for he was stripped for work), and threw himself into the sea. But the other disciples came in the little boat, for they were not far from the land, but about one hundred yards away, dragging the net full of fish. So when they got out on the land, they saw a charcoal fire already laid and fish placed on it, and bread. Jesus said to them, "Bring some of the fish which you have now caught." Simon Peter went up and drew the net to land, full of large fish, a hundred and fifty-three, and although there were so many, the net was

not torn. Jesus said to them, "Come and have breakfast."
(John 21:7–12)

Notice that the Lord, the one who had been offended by
Peter and the other disciples, initiated their restoration. Many
Christians, having failed to love the Lord as they ought, drift
away from Him in shame over their sin. But all believers
need to realize that their Savior is eager for them to return
to Him and be restored to fellowship. In Jeremiah 31:3 the
Lord says, "I have loved you with an everlasting love." Nothing can separate us from the love of Christ, not even our own
disobedience or our failure to love Him as we should. We can
be thankful for His love, which is unending and will reach
out to recover us.

Those who become complacent about their failure, however, and don't desire to restore their relationship to Christ
become comfortable with a superficial brand of Christianity
that avoids the priorities of God's kingdom. If that becomes
true of you, joy and peace are gone and God won't bless
you, but He may bring you under His chastening hand. Peter
wanted restoration.

After serving breakfast to the disciples, Jesus said to Simon
Peter, "Simon, son of John, do you love Me more than these?"
(John 21:15). The Greek word translated "love" is the familiar
agapao, which is the highest kind of love, the noblest kind of

devotion. It is the love of the will, not the emotions or feelings. It chooses to love.

By asking Peter if he supremely loved Him more than "these," Jesus may have been referring to the other disciples or to the trappings of his former life—his boat, his nets, and life on the sea as a fisherman. Jesus confronted Peter about his priorities: Did he love Christ more than his own life—more than his own plans, desires, and pleasures?

Peter's response was a carefully measured one: "Yes, Lord; You know that I love You" (v. 15). We see a different word for "love" in Peter's response: *phileo*, which refers to tender affection. It seems Peter couldn't claim *agapao* for Christ; that would have been blatant hypocrisy when measured against his behavior. The Lord then told him, "Tend My lambs" (v. 15). That command was a direct reminder to Peter that he was no longer a fisherman; he was now a shepherd of God's sheep.

Our Lord wasn't finished with Peter: "He said to him again a second time, 'Simon, son of John, do you love Me?' He said to Him, 'Yes, Lord; You know that I love You.' He said to him, 'Shepherd My sheep.' He said to him the third time, 'Simon, son of John, do you love Me?'" (vv. 16–17). On this third occasion, Jesus used the word for "love" that Peter had used—*phileo*. Thus Jesus was even questioning Peter's affection for Him. "Peter was grieved because He said to him the third time, 'Do you love Me?' And he said to Him, 'Lord, You know all things; You know that I love You.' Jesus said to him, 'Tend My sheep'" (v. 17).

It seems apparent that to coincide with Peter's three denials, three times Jesus questioned the validity of Peter's love for Him. As was true for Peter, the depth of our love for Christ must be demonstrated by our obedience. The test of love is not emotion or sentiment; the ultimate proof is in our obedience to Him.

Having established love as the most important ingredient in restoring their relationship, Christ delineated a closely related component:

> "Truly, truly, I say to you, when you were younger, you used to gird yourself and walk wherever you wished; but when you grow old, you will stretch out your hands [be put to death on a cross] and someone else will gird you, and bring you where you do not wish to go." Now this He said, signifying by what kind of death he would glorify God. (vv. 18–19)

There is always a cost attached to loving Christ, and that is a willingness to sacrifice for Him. Here Jesus was prophesying the martyrdom Peter would face. But He was also informing him that a necessary aspect of their relationship was Peter's willingness to give his life for Christ.

Jesus Himself identified the supreme mark of love: "Greater love has no one than this, that one lay down his life for his friends" (15:13). Whatever you are willing to sacrifice in your life for Christ is evidence of the depth of your love. Whatever you are unwilling to sacrifice will expose the shallowness of your love.

Jesus's last command for Peter was, "Follow Me!" (21:19, 22). Our Lord's restoration of Peter was now complete, and it ended with a command—one that Peter would obey. The time came when the apostle would not deny his Lord or disobey Him—and he was executed for it. Tradition says he was crucified upside down.

When the Lord is the priority of our lives, we will be willing to obey Him and thus prove our love to Him. But it doesn't come easily. Thomas Vincent appropriately wrote:

> Let your love show itself in the willingness of your obedience. Serve the Lord with a willing and ready mind, with alacrity and cheerfulness of spirit, looking upon the service of Christ as your honor, and esteeming every duty as your privilege. If you have any constraints upon obedience, let them be constraints of love, as 2 Corinthians 5:14. If you are forced to obey Christ, let there be no violence but the violence of love; if you are dragged to duty, let it be with no other cords than the cords of love. Let love be the spur and goad to prick you forward that you may not only walk but run in the ways of Christ's commandments with an enlarged heart.[1]

Daily Challenge

If you are ever going to have a meaningful relationship with your Lord and Savior—if you are ever going to return to your first love—you must begin by obeying Him. There are no shortcuts. Through our final three days we'll look at some of the ways Scripture encourages and motivates believers to do just that.

Day 29

In Pursuit
of Our First Love

Not that I have already obtained it or have already become perfect, but I press on so that I may lay hold of that for which also I was laid hold of by Christ Jesus. Brethren, I do not regard myself as having laid hold of it yet; but one thing I do: forgetting what lies behind and reaching forward to what lies ahead, I press on toward the goal for the prize of the upward call of God in Christ Jesus.

Philippians 3:12–14

What was the *it* to which the apostle Paul referred in the passage above, the goal and prize for which he strove so relentlessly? It was his relationship with Christ, the passion of his life: "that I may know Him and the power of His resurrection and the fellowship of His sufferings, being conformed to His death; in order that I may attain to the resurrection from the dead" (vv. 10–11). By comparing his pursuit of Christ to a lifelong race, he acknowledged that he would never completely achieve his goal short of heaven. Yet he pressed on.

Are you daily stretching forward toward a deeper relationship with Jesus? Or have you dropped out of the race, abandoning your first love? The only way to get back in the race is to "remember from where you have fallen, and repent and do the deeds you did at first" (Rev. 2:5).

That's what we have been endeavoring to do throughout this book. We have focused the major portion of it on what our beloved Savior and Lord has done and is doing for us. In the previous two days we looked at the apostle Peter's denial of Christ and his subsequent repentance and restoration to love, ending with our Lord's command to "Follow Me!" It is to that command we turn our attention in these concluding days. To "do the deeds you did at first," you must understand that your allegiance and love to Christ demand a lifelong commitment. As our Lord Himself said, "No one, after putting his hand to the plow and looking back, is fit for the kingdom of God" (Luke 9:62).

To Paul, the Christian life was a permanent pursuit of Christ—every day entering into a deeper and richer relationship with Him. He did not rest on all that he had been given in Christ (see Phil. 3:7–11). On the contrary, he had a humble, honest assessment of his own imperfection: "not that I have already obtained it, or have already become perfect" (v. 12). Our spiritual race begins with a sense of dissatisfaction—there's no reason to even begin the race without it. F. B. Meyer wisely observed that "self-dissatisfaction lies at the root of our noblest achievements."[1]

If you are to renew your first love, you must begin your pursuit of Christ the same way Paul did—with the awareness that you have much learning and growing to do. Once you start, there are several principles you need to apply as you pursue Him.

Considering who Christ is and what He has done for us, our effort should not be less than Paul's, who said, "I press on so that I may lay hold of that for which also I was laid hold of by Christ Jesus" (v. 12). The Greek word translated "press on" (*dioko*) was used of a sprinter who ran aggressively. That was the kind of effort Paul exerted—he ran to Christ with all his might, straining every spiritual muscle to win the prize (see 1 Cor. 9:24–27). The writer of Hebrews encouraged us to "lay aside every encumbrance and the sin which so easily entangles us, and let us run with endurance the race that is set before us" (Heb. 12:1). As Christians, there's only one race we ought to be running.

No one is going to put forth that kind of effort, however, unless there is some reward at the end. For Paul, and us as well, it is "that for which also I was laid hold of by Christ Jesus" (Phil. 3:12). Paul's prize, and ours, is the very purpose God had in saving us: "Whom He foreknew, He also predestined to become conformed to the image of His Son" (Rom. 8:29; see also 2 Thess. 2:14). God saved us so that we might become like Christ—our first love—and that should be our lifelong pursuit.

Christians must concentrate on attaining the goal of Christlikeness and not get distracted by worldly attractions and temptations. Paul was well aware of those dangers: "I do not regard myself as having laid hold of [Christlikeness] yet; but one thing I do: [forget] what lies behind and [reach] forward to what lies ahead" (Phil. 3:13). Paul was consumed with only one purpose in his life: "the prize of the upward call of God in Christ Jesus" (v. 14). That prize is being made like Christ (see 1 John 3:2).

Regaining our first love and focusing on Christ calls for two attitudes. First, we must forget the past. When we run the spiritual race in pursuit of Christ, the past is completely irrelevant. Our successes and failures in the past are insignificant to the present, let alone the future. We can't evaluate our usefulness by our former virtuous deeds and achievements in ministry; neither should we be debilitated by past sins and failures.

And second, we must reach for the goal. Instead of looking back, a good runner is always "reaching forward to what lies ahead" (Phil. 3:13). The Greek word for "reaching forward" is *epekteino*, and it refers to an intense stretching to the limit of one's capacity. Commentator William Hendricksen writes, "The verb . . . pictures the runner straining every nerve and muscle as he keeps on running with all his might toward the goal, his hand stretched out as if to grasp it."[2] Do you have that kind of concentration in your desire to become like Christ?

Paul was highly motivated in his pursuit of Christ: "I press on toward the goal for the prize of the upward call of God in Christ Jesus" (v. 14). He was motivated by spiritual matters; he was not caught up in material comforts and worldly pursuits. His goal was to be like Christ, and he would receive his reward when God's upward call came. Paul fought the battles, ran the race, and guarded the faith because of his love for Christ (see 2 Tim. 4:7–8). He did so because he longed for the day when he would be like Him completely. Christlikeness is both the goal and the prize we pursue.

Preoccupation with the world and material possessions serves no worthwhile purpose for Christians. Such a pursuit will only divert us from our proper motivation, which is to be like Christ.

Pursuit of Christ is objective, not subjective. It is not a mystical experience but an exposure to the truth about Christ revealed in the Bible. The knowledge of Christ is gained and enriched only in the Scripture that speaks of Him. The Bible is the mirror in which His glory is reflected. Paul said, "We all, with unveiled face, beholding as in a mirror the glory of the Lord, are being transformed into the same image from glory to glory" (2 Cor. 3:18).

Every believer ought to have the attitude that he or she is not perfect (see Phil. 3:15). Those who have that perspective regarding their spirituality will be ready to respond positively to God's correction. But rest assured, if you have the wrong attitude about your spirituality, if you're content with the current level of your spiritual growth, then God will reveal your true condition. Sometimes the Lord will bring chastening into our lives when we have lost the right perspective (see Heb. 12:5–11). At other times He will bring trials into our lives to reveal our true condition and to build and strengthen our faith and trust in Him (see James 1:2, 4).

Christlikeness cannot be reached with intermittent effort—it is an ongoing pursuit. So Paul says, "Let us keep living by that same standard to which we have attained" (Phil. 3:16). The Greek verb translated "keep living" refers to walking in line. Christians must stay in line spiritually and keep moving forward toward the goal of Christlikeness.

Daily Challenge

One summer I had the opportunity to visit Europe and in particular the Alps. At the foot of one of those majestic mountains is a famous gravestone. Underneath the individual's name the epitaph reads, "He died climbing." That ought to be our attitude as we pursue Christ. We ought to be in the process of pursuing Him when He calls us home.

Day 30
Focusing
on the Finish

Therefore if you have been raised up with Christ, keep seeking
the things above, where Christ is, seated at the right hand of
God. Set your mind on the things above, not on the things that
are on earth. For you have died and your life is hidden with
Christ in God. When Christ, who is our life, is revealed, then
you also will be revealed with Him in glory.

Colossians 3:1–4

Home is the Christian's focus because that is the end of the
race. To encourage the Philippian believers in their pursuit of
Christ, Paul said, "Our citizenship is in heaven, from which

also we eagerly wait for a Savior, the Lord Jesus Christ" (Phil. 3:20). As we look to the finish line, four great realities must occupy our minds: (1) we focus on our Lord who is in heaven, (2) we anticipate His coming to take us there, (3) we await our glorious transformation, and (4) we long expectantly for our divine inheritance.

In our pursuit of Christ, our track, as it were, is upward. It may begin on earth, but it ends in heaven, "where Christ is, seated at the right hand of God" (Col. 3:1). As we run in pursuit of Him, we are no longer being "conformed to this world," but we are being "transformed by the renewing of [our minds]" (Rom. 12:2).

Preoccupation with heavenly reality is the hallmark of true spirituality. It is only when we rise above the world that we learn to fix our minds on heavenly realities. Our blessings are in heaven, Christ is there, and we, through our union with Him in His resurrection, exist in the heavenly realm (see Eph. 1:3, 20; 2:6). Because we "have been raised up with Christ" (Col. 3:1), we are alive to the realities of the divine realm. When we were saved, the world ceased to be our home. We now have "our citizenship . . . in heaven" (Phil. 3:20).

The Greek word translated "citizenship" is used only in this verse and refers to a colony of foreigners. That certainly is true of Christians. We are the citizens of a place that is foreign to this world—heaven.

In Colossians 3:1 Paul said that we are to "keep seeking the things above." Preoccupation with the eternal realities that are ours in Christ is to be the pattern of the believer's life. Jesus put it this way: "Seek first His kingdom and His righteousness, and all these things will be added to you" (Matt. 6:33).

Our preoccupation with heaven will govern our earthly responses. When we are preoccupied with the One who reigns there, we will view the things, people, and events of this world through His eyes and with an eternal perspective. As we keep our focus on the heavenlies, we will live out our heavenly values in this world to the glory of God.

The thoughts of heaven that ought to fill our minds must derive from Scripture. The Bible is the only reliable source of knowledge about the character of God and the values of heaven. In it we learn about the things that should occupy our thoughts (see Phil. 4:8). As such heavenly values dominate our minds, they will produce godly behavior and make us more like the Christ we love (see 2 Cor. 3:18).

The more we love Him, the more we love His appearing (see 2 Tim. 4:8). We look forward to the day when Christ comes to take us home. "We eagerly wait for a Savior, the Lord Jesus Christ" (Phil. 3:20). When Christ returns for us, the race is over. Thus the anticipation of our Lord's return is a great source of spiritual motivation, accountability, and security.

Knowing that Jesus is coming provides tremendous motivation in reaching for the prize, because we'll want to be ready when He comes. We find motivation in the hope of one day being rewarded by Christ and hearing, "Well done, good and faithful slave . . . enter into the joy of your master" (Matt. 25:23).

Christ's return also provides us with accountability. We know that "each one of us will give account of himself to God" (Rom. 14:12) and that "if any man's work is burned up, he will suffer loss" (1 Cor. 3:15). That accountability alone ought to keep us pursuing Christ.

We can also rest secure in the fact of Christ's imminent return. In John 6:39 Jesus says, "This is the will of Him who sent Me, that of all that He has given Me I lose nothing, but raise it up on the last day."

Christ's return is not just an event in God's plan; it is the fulfillment of our lifelong desire. We eagerly anticipate the day when finally we will be in the presence of the One who has been the object of our love.

Paul says that when Christ returns, He "will transform the body of our humble state into conformity with the body of His glory" (Phil. 3:21). We look forward to His coming because we desire to be transformed. We long to be free from our sinful flesh and be perfect like Christ (see Rom. 8:23). Although we have been made a new creation in the inner man, that inner man is incarcerated in unredeemed flesh. Our fallen humanness and its lusts remain with us. The new creation within us longs to be liberated from the sin that remains.

If we die anytime before Christ comes for His own, our bodies go into the grave. Our spirits, however, immediately go to be with the Lord (see 2 Cor. 5:8; Phil. 1:23). Our bodies then await the second coming of Christ. At that time He will raise them all (see 1 Thess. 4:16) and transform them.

When God transforms our bodies, He will redesign and refashion them into ones adapted to an eternal, holy heaven. We will then be like Christ after His resurrection (see Phil. 3:21). We know that "when He appears, we will be like Him, because we will see Him just as He is" (1 John 3:2). God not only has saved us from hell and given us heaven but also will make us like His Son.

When we die, our spirits are instantly perfected. When Christ returns, our bodies are raised and transformed to be like Christ as holy instruments for worship and service. We will never again have an evil impulse or an errant motive. Our minds and hearts will be filled with the pure light of God's truth and undiluted love, joy, peace, and goodness. We ought to long for that with all our hearts.

On the day we enter fully into the Father's eternal heavenly kingdom, we will receive our promised inheritance (see Eph. 1:11). Our heavenly Father's resources are limitless, so our spiritual inheritance is limitless. God has appointed Jesus

Christ the "heir of all things" (Heb. 1:2), and because we are fellow heirs with Him (see Rom. 8:17), we will receive all that He receives!

On that day we will sit on the heavenly throne with Christ and rule there with Him (see Rev. 3:21), bearing forever the very image of our Savior and Lord (see 1 Cor. 15:49). In His great high priestly prayer, Jesus spoke to His Father of the incredible and staggering truth that everyone who believes in Him will be one with Him and will share His full glory: "The glory which You have given Me I have given to them; that they may be one, just as We are one" (John 17:22). It is not that we will become gods but that we will receive, by our joint inheritance with Christ, all the blessings and grandeur that God has.

Daily Challenge

One day everything on earth will perish, because the whole earth is defiled and corrupted. By great and marvelous contrast, however, one day every believer will "obtain an inheritance which is imperishable and undefiled and will not fade away" (1 Pet. 1:4). It is that very inheritance that is "reserved in heaven" for us. What a wonderful prize awaits us when we cross the finish line in pursuit of our glorious Lord and Savior.

Day 31
Training
for the Race

Discipline yourself for the purpose of godliness; for bodily discipline is only of little profit, but godliness is profitable for all things, since it holds promise for the present life and also for the life to come.

1 Timothy 4:7–8

When I was in college, I had the privilege of being a member of the school's track and field team. I performed best in the sprints, and occasionally the quarter mile. One of my favorite races was the mile relay. Of all the races we ran, the one I remember best is one we didn't win.

The race started wonderfully—our first runner ran such a great opening quarter-mile leg that, as he passed the baton to me, we were tied for the lead. I ran as hard as I could, hoping to at least maintain our position if not put us in front. As I passed the baton to our third runner, we were in first place. I thought we had an excellent chance to win—our fourth runner was especially fast.

Our third runner took off around the first curve and down the back stretch, holding on to our lead. And then the unthinkable happened. He stopped suddenly, walked off the track, and sat down on the grass. I ran over to him, thinking that he must have pulled a muscle. When I reached him, he didn't look like he was in pain, so I asked what was wrong. I'll never forget his reply. All he said was, "I don't know—I just didn't feel like running."

Sadly, many Christians are like that runner. Somewhere along the way they stopped pursuing a deep, loving relationship with Christ, walked off His path of righteousness, and sat down to rest in their own self-righteousness and the ease of worldly pleasures. In so doing they left their first love. The risen Jesus speaks to us, just as He did to the Ephesian Christians: "Remember from where you have fallen, and repent and do the deeds you did at first" (Rev. 2:5).

Maybe you've been out of the race and you're ready to join back in. Whether you departed from the Lord's path a long time ago, or just earlier today, He welcomes you back. Or maybe you're actively pursuing Him—perhaps jogging, or running, or in an all-out sprint. Every athlete, from the out-of-shape beginner to the finely tuned defending champion, must train continually. In the same way all believers need to be in constant training because our race is lifelong. Thomas Vincent's book, *The True Christian's Love to the Unseen Christ*, offers nine principles that we should always be practicing in our pursuit of Christ.[1] They make a fitting climax to this study, because they encapsulate the very deeds that Christ would have us repeat (see Rev. 2:5).

Direction 1: "Be much in contemplation of Christ."[2] If you are to ever return to your first love, your first priority is to meditate on Christ. Don't let one day go by without taking the time to dwell on Him: on who He is, what He has done, and what He is doing for you. Vincent suggested, "Spend time in secret retirement, and there think and think again of the superlative excellencies and perfections which are in Christ's person; how wonderful and matchless His love is."[3]

Direction 2: "Be much in reading and studying the Scriptures."[4] The Bible is God's Word to you. It is where we find everything we need to know about our great Lord and Savior. Paul said that we are to "let the word of Christ richly dwell within [us]" (Col. 3:16). To not feed on its truths every day is like going without food for a day (see Matt. 4:4).

Direction 3: "Be much in prayer to God for this love."[5] Jesus said, "How much more will your Father who is in heaven give what is good to those who ask Him!" (7:11). I can't think of anything better than having supreme love toward Christ, and God will certainly give that to us if we ask Him for it sincerely. Vincent said, "Be often at the throne of grace upon your knees, and there humbly acknowledge if not the lack, yet the weakness, of your love to Christ. Bewail your sins which dampen your affections, and earnestly request that He would work your hearts unto a strong love."[6]

Direction 4: "Get much faith."[7] This directive goes hand in hand with prayer. The writer of Hebrews said, "Faith is the assurance of things hoped for, the conviction of things not seen" (Heb. 11:1). Peter said of Christ, "Though you have not seen Him, you love Him" (1 Pet. 1:8). We can apprehend Christ in no other way but by faith, thus that is the only way we can truly love Him. Vincent said, "Such as are without any faith are without any love; such as have but feeble faith have but weak love; and such as have the strongest faith have the strongest love."[8]

Direction 5: "Labor for much of the Spirit; labor for much of the light of the Spirit."[9] The only way to truly love Christ is to "be filled with the Spirit" (Eph. 5:18), a state that requires frequent renewing. Jesus said: "I will ask the Father, and He will give you another Helper, that He may be with you forever; that is the Spirit of truth" (John 14:16–17).

Direction 6: "Labor for clear evidences of His love unto you," to which Vincent added, "The full, well-grounded persuasions of Christ's love to you will, above all, heighten your love to Christ."[10] If you lack the assurance of your salvation, examine your life to make sure you are saved. But if you are a true Christian, don't doubt our Lord's love, for Paul said, "God demonstrates His own love toward us, in that while we were yet sinners, Christ died for us" (Rom. 5:8).

Direction 7: "Get much hatred of sin and, accordingly, watch, pray, strive, and fight against sin as the worst of evils, as that which so much displeases your Lord."[11] When you do sin, go to the Lord and confess it so that you might experience the joy of restoration. Vincent encouraged us further:

> Disturb sin as much as you can; wage war every day with your remaining lusts. Let no day pass over your heads without giving some blows, some thrusts and wounds to sin. . . . Particularly, take heed of inordinate love to the world and the things in the world, the prevalence of which love will dampen your love to Christ. By how much more the world gets of your love, by so much the less Christ will have it.[12]

Direction 8: "Associate yourselves most with those that have most love unto Christ."[13] Simply stated, follow godly examples. Paul said, "Join in following my example, and observe those who walk according to the pattern you have in us" (Phil. 3:17).

Direction 9: "Be much in exercise of this love; hereby it is increased and heightened."[14] This last directive takes us back to the beginning. If we are to continually pursue Christ, we must be pursuing Him and practicing each of these directives every day. In every activity, in every contact, and in every thought, Christ is to be your focus. When you make Him your priority, you encourage the faithful and convict the unregenerate. When you love Christ with all your heart, soul, and strength, God is glorified.

Daily Challenge

Some years ago I wrote a song about my desire to be like Christ. I hope it expresses the desire of your heart.

> *O to be like Thee, dear Jesus, my plea,*
> *Just to know Thou art formed fully in me.*
> *On with Thy beauty, Lord, off with my sin,*
> *Fixed on Thy glory, Thy likeness to win.*
> *O to be like Thee, Thine image display,*
> *This is the Spirit's work day after day.*
> *Glory to glory, transformed by His grace,*
> *Till in Thy presence I stand face-to-face.*
> *O to be like Thee, Thou lover of men,*
> *Gracious and gentle, compassionate friend,*
> *Merciful Savior, such kindness and care*
> *Are only mine when Your likeness I share.*
>
> J.M.

Notes

Day 1 First Love

1. Thomas Vincent, *The True Christian's Love to the Unseen Christ* (Ligonier, PA: Soli Deo Gloria, 1993), 1.

2. Ibid., 1–2.

Day 2 No Mere Man

1. John Owen, *The Glory of Christ* (Chicago: Moody Press, 1949), 25–26.

Day 5 Chosen in Christ

1. D. Martyn Lloyd-Jones, *God's Ultimate Purpose: An Exposition of Ephesians 1:1 to 23* (Grand Rapids: Baker, 1979), 94.

Day 7 God's Plan from Eternity Past

1. J. I. Packer, *Evangelism and the Sovereignty of God* (Chicago: InterVarsity Press, 1961), 16–17.

Day 8 The God-Man

1. C. S. Lewis, "The Grand Miracle," *Miracles* (New York: Macmillan, 1960), 111–12.

2. See William Barclay, *The Letters to the Philippians, Colossians, and Thessalonians* (Philadelphia: Westminster, 1976), 35.

3. James Hope Moulton and George Milligan, *The Vocabulary of the Greek Testament* (Grand Rapids: Eerdmans, 1930), 417.

Day 9 In the Likeness of Men

1. See William Hendricksen, *New Testament Commentary: Exposition of Philippians* (Grand Rapids: Baker, 1979), 110.

Day 10 Even Death on a Cross

1. Benjamin Warfield, *The Person and Work of Christ* (Philadelphia: Presbyterian and Reformed Press, 1950), 563–64.

Day 11 Our Desperate Need

1. Leon Morris, *The Cross in the New Testament* (Grand Rapids: Eerdmans, 1965), 410.

Day 12 Our Loving Substitute

1. Morris, *Cross in the New Testament*, 410.

2. Ibid., 405.

Day 14 Righteous through Justification

1. For an in-depth treatment of justification, please see my book *The Gospel According to the Apostles* (Nashville: Nelson, 2000).

Day 17 The One Eternal Sacrifice

1. Benjamin B. Warfield, *The Works of Benjamin B. Warfield: Biblical Doctrines*, vol. 2 (New York: Oxford University Press, 1929), 435.

Day 19 Our Risen Lord

1. Charles Hodge, *Commentary on the Epistle to the Romans* (Grand Rapids: Eerdmans, 1983), 129.

2. Benjamin B. Warfield, *The Saviour of the World* (Carlisle, PA: Banner of Truth Trust, 1991), 210–12. Emphasis in original.

Day 20 Our King Takes His Throne

1. D. Martyn Lloyd-Jones, *The Life of Joy, An Exposition of Philippians 1 and 2* (Grand Rapids: Baker, 1989), 153–54.

2. William Hendricksen, *Philippians, Colossians and Philemon* (Grand Rapids: Baker, 1962), 11. Emphasis in original.

Day 21 Every Knee and Every Tongue

1. Lloyd-Jones, *Life of Joy*, 153–54.

Day 22 Our Sympathetic High Priest

1. J. B. Cranfill, *A Quest for Souls* (Dallas: Texas Baptist Book House, 1917), np.

Day 23 Our Advocate with the Father

1. Peter Lewis, *The Glory of Christ* (London: Hodder & Stoughton, 1992), 387–88. Emphasis in original.

Day 24 Following Our Lord in Suffering

1. Lehman Strauss, *The Second Person* (New York: Loizeaux Brothers, 1951), 113–14.

2. Ibid., 114.

Day 25 Our Lord's Response to Suffering

1. Bishop Hugh Latimer, as cited in Harold S. Darby, *Hugh Latimer* (London: Epworth, 1953), 237.

2. Ibid., 247.

3. Charles Haddon Spurgeon, as cited in Tom Carter, *Spurgeon at His Best* (Grand Rapids: Baker, 1988), 202. Emphasis added.

Day 26 Love and Obedience

1. Vincent, *True Christian's Love to the Unseen Christ*, 24–25.

2. Ibid., 30–31. Emphasis in original.

Day 28 Returning to Love

1. Vincent, *True Christian's Love to the Unseen Christ*, 87.

Day 29 In Pursuit of Our First Love

1. F. B. Meyer, *The Epistle to the Philippians: A Devotional Commentary* (Grand Rapids: Baker, 1952), 175.

2. Hendricksen, *New Testament Commentary: Exposition of Philippians*, 173.

Day 31 Training for the Race

1. Vincent, *True Christian's Love to the Unseen Christ*, 75.

2. Ibid.

3. Ibid.

4. Ibid., 78.
5. Ibid., 79.
6. Ibid., 80.
7. Ibid., 81.
8. Ibid.
9. Ibid., 82.
10. Ibid.
11. Ibid., 83.
12. Ibid., 84.
13. Ibid.
14. Ibid., 85.

John MacArthur is the pastor-teacher of Grace Community Church in Sun Valley, California, president of Master's College & Seminary, and featured teacher for the Grace to You media ministry. Weekly telecasts and daily radio broadcasts of *Grace to You* are seen and heard by millions worldwide. John has also written several bestselling books including *The MacArthur Study Bible*, *The Gospel According to Jesus*, The New Testament Commentary series, *Twelve Ordinary Men*, and *The Truth War*. He and his wife, Patricia, have four married children and fifteen grandchildren.

PULPIT OF **JOHN CALVIN** | ST. PIERRE CATHEDRAL | GENEVA, SWITZERLAND

WE PREACH **CHRIST**

THE MASTER'S SEMINARY

ALSO BY JOHN MacARTHUR

Solid Biblical Teaching for Today